"Clear, compelling, and exciting. Ellen provides a much-needed reminder that local churches living in and by the power of God are the way He displays His glory and goodness to a broken world."

ALISTAIR BEGG, Bible Teacher on Truth for Life;
Bestselling Author of *Pray Big* and *Truth For Life*

"Relaying the true-life accounts of simple believers who labor in small, dark corners of the earth, Ellen shows us once again how 'weakness and humility' open the way for God to perform His most powerful, kingdom-shaping work. The faith-forging stories you will read in this exceptional book will stir you—as they've stirred me—to roll up our sleeves and do the hard, modest labor that will impact our communities for Christ."

JONI EARECKSON TADA, Joni and Friends
International Disability Center

"The apostle Paul said that God's promises are 'yes' and 'amen.' One of His promises was to build the church, and, as Ellen Vaughn describes in these pages, He has. The stories she tells should inspire and encourage us to *be* the church where He has placed us, resting in the promise that 'the gates of hell shall not prevail,' but the church certainly will."

JOHN STONESTREET, President of The Colson Center

"When Ellen Vaughn writes something, I read it—no question. What she writes is never boring. She makes history come alive—not just as facts or a compelling narrative but as a story she genuinely understands and helps you understand too, and in a way that points straight to the hand of God moving through it all. *What Jesus Started* is a rich, compelling, and beautifully written book that celebrates the local church as God's primary instrument for changing the world. It will inform you, stir you, and challenge you to live differently for Christ."

GREG LAURIE, Pastor at Harvest Christian Fellowship
and Evangelist for Harvest Crusades

"Jesus said, 'I will build my church, and the gates of hell shall not prevail against it.' In this remarkable book, Ellen Vaughn shows how He continues to do that. The stories she shares are eye-opening and soul-stirring. I hope this book will be widely read and that the Spirit will stir us all to prayer and action."

CAROLYN LACEY, Author of *Say the Right Thing*

"Jesus came to build His church, but we've often settled for building a crowd. If you're longing for more than just 'church as usual,' the real-life stories in this book will stir your faith and call you back to the movement Jesus started."

MIKE KELSEY, Lead Pastor at McLean Bible Church

"*What Jesus Started* will help rejuvenate a faith grown stale or one coddled by Western comforts. Ellen not only writes with the pen of a poet and the wisdom of a sage but with a passion for the local church. She calls us back to our thrilling roots. This is a book the church needs to read. And as we do, we'll discover it's the one we've wanted to read for a long time."

KELLY MINTER, Bible Teacher and Author of *The Blessed Life*

"Does your faith feel stagnant or small? Do you long to hear of God's miraculous works in ordinary individuals across the world? Reading these true stories will set your heart ablaze with a fresh perspective on how very big and how very good our God is. In our broken world it brings very good news."

SUSAN ALEXANDER YATES, Speaker and Author

"Ellen has captured stories that expand and challenge us all. I was blessed to travel with Ellen when she collected many of the stories in this book, and I can attest that there are thousands more that could be told! The Spirit of the living God is working in powerful ways to continue to build what Jesus started."

JANICE ROSSER ALLEN, CEO and President of ICM

New York Times Bestselling Author

ELLEN VAUGHN

WHAT JESUS STARTED

The WORLD-CHANGING POWER *of* THE LOCAL CHURCH

thegoodbook COMPANY

What Jesus Started

Published by:
The Good Book Company

thegoodbook.com | thegoodbook.co.uk
thegoodbook.com.au | thegoodbook.co.nz

Every book published by The Good Book Company has been written by a human author and edited by a human editor. While AI tools are sometimes used to assist with research and support certain processes, all content has been created by a human author and thoroughly checked by our editorial team to ensure it is biblically faithful and pastorally wise.

Published in association with the literary agency of Wolgemuth & Wilson.

Cover design by Studio Gearbox | Design and art direction by André Parker

ISBN: 9781802544442 | JOB-008598 | Printed in India

CONTENTS

To Patti Bryce,
life-long best friend and fellow pilgrim on the great journey

Soli Deo Gloria

Now the eleven disciples went to Galilee, to the mountain to which Jesus had directed them. And when they saw him they worshiped him, but some doubted. And Jesus came and said to them,
"All authority in heaven and on earth has been given to me. Go therefore and make disciples of all nations, baptizing them in the name of the Father and of the Son and of the Holy Spirit, teaching them to observe all that I have commanded you. And behold, I am with you always, to the end of the age."

MATTHEW 28:16-20

But you will receive power when the Holy Spirit has come upon you, and you will be my witnesses in Jerusalem and in all Judea and Samaria, and to the end of the earth.

ACTS 1:8

Part 1

WHAT JESUS STARTED

Chapter 1

WHISPERS FROM THE EAST

And a vision appeared to Paul in the night: a man of Macedonia was standing there, urging him and saying, "Come over to Macedonia and help us." And when Paul had seen the vision, immediately we sought to go on into Macedonia, concluding that God had called us to preach the gospel to them.

ACTS 16:9-10

Kazakhstan, the largest landlocked country in the world, is a mystery to many in the West. It's bordered by Russia, the Caspian Sea, Turkmenistan, Uzbekistan, the Kyrgyz Republic, and China. It's home to snowy mountains, crystal lakes, and endless steppes whose grasses sway in the wind.

If you look hard enough, you can see into the past, when Kazakhstan was a land of sultans and great khans. Kazakhstan saw wars, invaders, and threats, but its pastoral nomads were rich in their own fierce culture.

In the 20th century, Kazakhstan became part of the Soviet Union, ruled by Joseph Stalin. His forced collectivization of farms caused massive starvation; one-fifth of Kazakhstan's people died.

In this context, Stalin, brutal dictator, provides the backdrop for the story of one small Kazakh woman named Gulshamal. In English, her name means "suffering flower." This gentle flower lived in a largely forgotten Kazakh area known by some as the "Land of the Outcasts." She outlived Stalin, and God used her as the tiniest of seeds for new hope that only He could plant.

It started with God moving in one of His friends—a hearty, Jesus-loving, exuberant bear of a man named Paul Hagelgans. Paul is from Kazakhstan; he served in the Russian army as a young man. His grandfather, a pastor, was murdered by Stalin's thugs. Paul learned of Jesus as a child and follows Him still.

I'll tell you later how I met him.

Many years ago, Paul saw a newspaper article about people who were suffering from leprosy in the former USSR. Curious because of Jesus' specific compassion for such sufferers, Paul researched further. He talked to a pastor who was interested in planting a church near a town now called Kyzylorda.

"Yes," the man told Paul. "There's a leprosy colony about 180 kilometers [112 miles] from that town. I've prayed for the people there, but I've never stopped in their village."

Paul Hagelgans is neither shy nor hesitant. He went to Kazakhstan's ministry of health. "I want to get a permit to visit the people in the leprosy colony," he told the officials there. They stared at him, now understanding that he was a crazy man. But Paul being Paul, he convinced them to give him a pass to visit the leprosy colony.

In March 1995, Paul and a group of fellow Christians arrived at the colony. It was then a closed zone where the government had sequestered all those in the country who had leprosy.

Paul and his small team met first with the medical staff, led by a man they called Uncle Volodia. Volodia had originally come from St. Petersburg as a young, gifted surgeon. His life's dream was to see the last person suffering from leprosy in Kazakhstan. When he arrived, the colony had 10,000 inhabitants; in 1995, there were only about 1,000 left.

Volodia gave permission for Paul and his colleagues to go from room to room in the area of the hospital that housed the most severe cases.

Thrilled to have visitors, the patients told Paul their life stories. He would ask if he could pray for them, and if they were open, share the unique hope found in Jesus Christ, friend of those with leprosy.

In one small room, a nurse had helped an elderly patient to sit up in her narrow hospital bed. The woman motioned with one clubbed hand for Paul to come in. She had thin, white hair trailing from a long piece of gauzy fabric wrapped around her head. She had wild gray eyebrows but only parts of her ears and remnants of her lips. She had no fingers, and shocking, empty sockets where her eyes should have been.

Her name was Gulshamal. She told Paul her story.

"When I was just a small girl in my village," she said, "men wearing uniforms brought a family to live with my family. It was during the Second World War, and the government had rounded up Germans from the western part of the Soviet Union. They sent the men to work in camps, and they sent the women to live and work in faraway places. I lived in a faraway place."

The Germans assigned to Gulshamal's house were a grandmother, a mother, and her little daughter, who was Gulshamal's age. The German girl picked up Kazakh quickly. Every night the girl's grandmother would tell her bedtime stories, and then every day, after the adults had gone to work in the fields, the German girl would tell them to Gulshamal.

Remembering those days so long ago, Gulshamal sighed. "Ah, those were beautiful stories! Every morning, I could not wait to hear the next one. Now I don't remember them all, but they all had one hero. His name was *Īsā Masīh*."

Paul recognized the name. The Arabic title for Jesus, the Christ.

Gulshamal and her playmate spent many months together. But one day men in Soviet uniforms came and rounded up the Germans. They were to be deported further into the icy bowels of the Soviet Union, many to their deaths in Siberia. Gulshamal never saw her friend again.

Time passed.

Gulshamal missed her friend desperately. She comforted herself over the years by rehearsing the beautiful stories she had been told. Eventually she became very ill. She developed discolored patches of skin, numbness, and muscle weakness. It was leprosy. Her toes and fingers shortened, then retracted. Parts of her body dropped away; her eyes failed.

Now I don't remember them all, but they all had one hero. His name was *Īsā Masīh*.

She gradually became worse, and in 1965 she was dropped off at the front gate of the leprosy colony. By 1995, Gulshamal was a frail stick of a woman who, true to her name, had suffered greatly. Her world had taken on the confines of the 8 x 10 foot room where she now lived. But still… she had held on to hope for all those decades—the hope first instilled in her by her little German friend.

"I remembered the stories!" she said to Paul. "I remembered how this *Īsā* was healing the sick people, even the ones with leprosy. I remembered that my German friend had told me that *Īsā* had come to save people from their sins. I knew I was a very big sinner. I remembered that this *Īsā* even died for the sins of the people. But then I remembered the best story of all:

how God had raised Him from the dead. How could that be?

"In the Soviet Union, it was not allowed to talk about *Īsā*. But even though I was stuck in this place, even though my eyes rotted away and I could no longer see, I was searching. Searching for God.

"And then I thought, what about all these other people around me? These poor sufferers! If what my friend told me is the truth, then what about them? So, I started praying to God that He would send someone from far away to tell all these people here the stories about *Īsā*."

Gulshamal raised her hands in the air, though she had no fingers. Sobs shook her face, though she had no eyes. "I have always remembered the stories of this man who healed the people with leprosy, gave sight to blind people, and forgave sins! I have been praying for 30 years… praying that someone would come to this forgotten place to tell the beautiful stories of *Īsā*, the one who loved the outcasts."

She paused, her sightless eye sockets turned toward Paul even as tears coursed down his ruddy cheeks. "And now," she said, "my prayer has been answered. *You have come!*"

The commonality of various communist regimes is their cruelty, whether exercised by Joseph Stalin in the former Soviet Union or by the revolutionary Pol Pot in southeast Asia.

In the aftermath of America's disastrous experience in Vietnam, communist forces took power in neighboring Cambodia. Led by the brutal revolutionary Pol Pot, the Khmer Rouge army entered the capital city of Phnom Penh. Pol Pot's soldiers destroyed highways, buildings, medical equipment, and hospitals. They burned books and eradicated every vestige of western technology and infrastructure. Their vision was for an agrarian state made up of workers and peasants, egalitarian to the core—except for those who held power and enjoyed privileges others did not.

Infrastructure aside, the regime's greatest destruction was reserved for its people. The Khmer Rouge marched Phnom Penh's two million citizens into the countryside. Pol Pot had long lists of "undesirables," such as doctors, monks, journalists, people who spoke French or wore eyeglasses, or those too young or too old to work for what Pol Pot called *Angka Loeu*, meaning "Organization on High."

As many as two million human beings—a quarter of the country's population—were beheaded, shot, bludgeoned, drowned, strangled, buried alive, or slowly tortured to death. Soldiers smashed babies against trees. Twenty thousand people were sent to Security Prison 21 for interrogation. Only seven survived.

The bodies rotted in mass graves, where their battered skulls endured to become the symbols of Pol Pot's "killing fields." Those who survived were sent to labor and reeducation camps, where everyone five and older was expected to work 16 hours a day. The communists killed those who could not meet production quotas. They obliterated schools and family structures. They rewarded children for allegiance to Pol Pot, or "Uncle," and educated them in the fine art of informing on their parents.

After four years of this brutal madness, Vietnamese forces invaded Cambodia. Pol Pot and his Khmer Rouge fled into the jungle. He was sentenced to death *in absentia* on genocide charges and finally died under detention by his own troops in 1998.

A year or so later, a Cambodian pastor I'll call Tuy Seng traveled to Kampong Tom province in the north of his country. As far as anyone knew, Pastor Seng was the first person to speak of Jesus in that isolated area. Most villagers cast their lot with Buddhism or ancestral worship. Christianity was unknown.

But when Pastor Seng arrived at one small village, the people welcomed him eagerly. They couldn't hear enough about Jesus. Most wanted to change their ways and follow Him.

Smiling, Pastor Seng asked the people why it seemed as if they'd been waiting for him to come.

An old woman shuffled to the front of the group. "We *have* been waiting," she said. "We have been waiting for you for 20 years. And now you have come!"

Then she told him this story.

After the Khmer Rouge took over Cambodia and remade its city centers in their own image, they pressed on into the countryside, destroying anything created with purpose and design—bridges, highways, hospitals, and human beings. It took time, but they pressed on into rural villages.

So it was that the soldiers had come to this hamlet 20 years earlier. Their technique was the same as it had been for countless communities, but for the people who lived there, the terror was new. The communists ravaged from hut to hut, ordering the villagers out. Those who resisted were killed at once; many died in front of their homes.

The rest were marched to a clearing behind the village. Their own farm tools were thrust into their hands.

"Now dig!" the soldiers shouted.

The villagers hacked the soil, trembling with the dark realization that they were digging their own mass grave. Some lost their nerve and tried to run. They were shot and dragged to the edge of the still shallow pit.

Hours passed. The people sweated and wept and dug, until finally the hole was deep enough. The soldiers shouted for them to turn and face the pit.

They braced themselves, waiting for the killing blows, knowing that the soldiers would bludgeon them to death rather than shoot them—why waste precious bullets on ordinary peasants?

The heavy, humid air lay still as the villagers began to cry out in the wail before death, when the heart's longing to live becomes a desperate plea for help. Some screamed to Buddha or to ancestors or to demon spirits. A few cried for their mothers.

Then one woman began to cry, intuitively, to one of her earliest memories—the faint echo of a story told her by her mother about the God who hung on a cross. She called out for that God. Surely the One who had suffered Himself might have compassion on those about to die. She cried for Him.

And suddenly the screams around her became one great wail as the entire village called out as one, crying for their lives to the God who hung on the cross.

They sobbed into the darkness of the pit before them.

Silence. A flicker of hope.

And then the people turned around, one by one by one.

The jungle was empty. The soldiers were gone.

And ever since that astounding day so long before, the people of that village had been waiting. Waiting for someone to come and tell them more—more about the God who hung on the cross.

Chapter 2

FISHBOWLS AND FIRST-CENTURY FAITH

Peter was filled with the Holy Spirit and told the nation's leaders and the elders … "Only Jesus has the power to save! His name is the only one in all the world that can save anyone."

ACTS 4:8, 12, CEV

These stories that I heard in Kazakhstan and Cambodia can stir up many things.

First, they sound foreign to many North American ears because, well, they are.

Second, they can sound to Christians like a plea for evangelism, with a tinge of guilt mixed in: *this* is why we must reach the three billion people around the world who have never heard the name of Jesus. The fields are white with harvest.

True, but my focus in telling these strange stories to myself and to you is to remind us of something more elemental: the absolute mystery and power of the gospel. Many of us have forgotten the main thing. There is *power* in the name of Jesus.

His gospel is not just a compendium of information, a list of tenets we check off if we agree, or a worldview we adopt for talking points. Christianity itself is not a political stance or a cultural nicety or an adjective for our social media profiles.

The gospel is a living story, dangerous, multidimensional, and infused by the Holy Spirit, who hovers all over this dark earth, whispering glory to God in places as hard as stone. Like remote jungles in southeast Asia or Stalin's USSR or India's Hindu strongholds or, as we'll see, in the libraries of Muslim extremists, or, dare we hope, even in the complacent comforts of 21st-century North America.

Throughout history, His name has endured. And so, against all odds, has His church.

If you reread the book of Acts with fresh eyes, the story of the church's beginnings takes your breath away. It's an account of an unlikely organic movement of diverse people—fishermen, tentmakers, small-business owners, political officials, slaves, and free men and women of all backgrounds who multiplied all over the world and changed the course of history. Noticeably missing from this new community were those who considered themselves "religious": those who were complacent, self-satisfied, self-defined, and assured of their own goodness.

Throughout history, His name has endured. And so, against all odds, has His church.

No, this unlikely community kept growing and growing, flowing with the Holy Spirit, continuing the work that Jesus had started.

In the New Testament, we see the Jesus story introduced: "all that Jesus began to do and teach."[1] Neither the Kingdom of God nor the Messiah Himself looked like what people

---

1 Acts 1:1.

had expected. Jesus Christ, the Messiah, was not a political king who would rescue the Jews from their pagan Roman oppressors but a suffering servant who gave His life for all who would receive Him, that they might have the power to become the sons and daughters of God.[2]

And in the book of Acts, we see the continuation of the surprising story—what Jesus *continued* to do, through the power of the Holy Spirit, growing His church made up of people from every tribe and nation, sinners who were thrilled that they could be swept up in the tsunami of God's grace because of the one Gulshamal called *Īsā malik*: Jesus, the Messiah.

Many of us in the West today are hungry for an organic movement of the power of the name of Jesus, like what happened in the days of the early church.

Many of us are weary, overwhelmed, and longing for supernatural transformation. We long for an authentic, exciting, and radically loving reality of church and Christian community in this angry world.

As I write, political polarization and demonization of the opposition have been the cacophonous norm for the past few years. Common courtesy took a sabbatical and never came back. Identity politics and culture wars fill every virtual space, as well as adolescent social media spats between people who are supposed to be grown-ups. Families are split as never before by differing political views, and it's the same in many churches. Protests, riots, mass shootings, crime, suffering at home and abroad. Wars, earthquakes, floods, and human injustice. Children bloodied and trafficked in the rubble of the Middle East, the former Soviet Union, and across Africa, Asia, Europe, North and South America, and every other place where human beings live.

---

2 John 1:12, RSV.

The news cycle overwhelms us with horror, then moves briskly on to the next headline, which may well involve a celebrity we just don't want to hear any more about.

Much has been written about the feelings of confusion, helplessness, and fatigue that such an environment can create. For many, the emotional exhaustion makes them more susceptible to numbing and isolating themselves in a privately curated cocoon of nice idols: comfort, convenience, and control.

Stay comfy and keep scrolling. *What do I want?* Maybe another golden retriever video will ease my boredom and anxiety, or if I learn how to make my own corn tortillas from scratch or how to build a tiny house in the backyard. Or what about another Amazon delivery? Or what about that lurking host of darker comfort substitutes?

But there's an opportunity here. The barrage of innocuous distractions and the bad, the ugly, and the lies can compel us to stop.

Stop. This status quo, both within me and around me, is shriveling my soul. God, show me the true, the good, and the beautiful.

I have seen that best in the midst of the ugly. Like Jesus' whisper of love to a leprosy sufferer in Kazakhstan. Or, as I'll relate later, the loveliness of churches opening their doors to those left homeless by the cruel war in Ukraine. The goodness of a hot bowl of borscht for a hungry and frightened child. The beauty of a shared meal and a vigorous hymn-sing on the floor of a dark, cramped apartment in Tajikistan, or of a sun-warmed bag of peanuts shared with former child soldiers outside a mud hut in northern Uganda. Those young believers had told me the story of their lives, and the fun beauty of our shared peanut fellowship came from the truth of the gospel: the liberating reality of God's blood-spattered forgiveness for us, all because of Jesus' sacrifice on the cross, and His explosive, ebullient resurrection from the gray ranks of the silent dead, so we can live too.

I've gotten to see such things because of an unusual opportunity.

> In this cultural moment of great weariness, dullness, and complacency among many in the church in the West, we can be refreshed and reminded of what is true and good by our brothers and sisters in the East and Global South.

Not too long after my husband Lee's death, I embarked on a series of journeys. I had just finished writing the second volume of my authorized biography of Elisabeth Elliot and was ready for something different. I'd also somehow remodeled parts of our home in that season, and I was anxious to remodel me. So "The Widow Vaughn," as Lee had insisted on calling me before he went off to Heaven, got on some airplanes and went forth to a variety of unlikely destinations.

I flew away in order to interview dozens of indigenous Christian leaders and laypeople. These were not just individuals; they were all part of local churches that were transforming their communities. I found myself in Ukraine, Moldova, India, Nepal, Rwanda, Brazil, Nepal, South Africa, Turkey, Zambia, Tajikistan, and Uganda. These pilgrimages enhanced what I had seen on prior similar journeys to Iraq, Egypt, Cuba, Cambodia, Romania, Peru, Vietnam, Colombia, China, Guatemala, El Salvador, Costa Rica, the Dominican Republic, and deep in the Amazon jungles of Ecuador.

There is nothing like getting out of one's own cultural fishbowl to break out of parochial paradigms. Also, swimming with my fellow fish abroad refreshed my love for and purpose in my own fishbowl, where God has placed me.

This is why I'm writing this book, including just a few of the many invigorating stories I heard abroad. I believe—in this cultural moment of great weariness, dullness, and complacency among many in the church in the West—we can be refreshed and reminded of what is true and good by our brothers and sisters in the East and Global South.

Western Christians habitually think in terms of Big Things, especially new and improved Big Things. Our itching ears are addicted to novelty. There can be a great energy in that tendency, but I just don't think now is the time to yearn for a new movement, for a new spiritual formula from some powerful social influencer, for a fresh, strategic start-up, or for some new, culture-changing realization that we just didn't think of until now.

It's time to remember what Jesus started 2,000 years ago: the new-covenant community of faith rooted in God's Old Testament revelation, His church.

It's time to reconnect to the old.

It's also time to think small. Not "How can we change the church in America?" But rather "Lord, what would you have me be and do in my particular church community, where I live?"

The phrasing of that question is important. Again, our gung-ho Western activism is tempted to start with "What would You have us *do*?" We are very good at programs and movements and action plans. But let's pull up the horses before we gallop off in all directions at once. The first question is "Who would You have us *be*?" or, more to the point, "Who are we, in You?" Our actions will always flow out of our identity. Being precedes doing.

So, who are we?

We live in a time when defining our own identity according to our own preference is a hallmark of our autonomous Western culture. This self-identification is much bigger than questions of sexuality and gender. It's the core of how we perceive everything.

Bluntly put, every follower of Jesus Christ has a unique identity that flows from God. That's because He made each one of us, knew us before we were formed *in utero*, and loves us with a love that will never let us go.

Over a cup of tea with a former Muslim sister in southwestern Turkey, she spontaneously spoke of this reality. As a Muslim, she said, "I saw Allah as a god of men, so why would a woman praise him? Then God showed me Himself. I understood that Jesus Christ is God, and my heart changed… like Isaiah, I said 'Here I am; whatever You want, use me.' Jesus changed my *identity*."

Being a Christian involves this crazy voluntary exchange: my will for His. My truth for His. My comfort for His cross. My preference for His power. I yield to Another because I believe He is actually God and that before I was even aware of Him, He knew me, saw me, loved me, and gave Himself for me. Because He first loved us, if we decide to follow Jesus, we love Him and sacrificially find our true selves in Him alone.

A thousand difficult but liberating ramifications, both individual and collective, flow from this exchange.

First, I follow Jesus as an individual, uniquely and specifically loved and saved to one day somehow stand on my own two celestial feet before Him.

But, in being grafted to Jesus, I am inextricably connected to His family. His church. I am not on my own. I am part of something much bigger than myself.

I am not the autonomous ruler of my own self-shaped kingdom but an intrinsic, irreplaceable part of a whole that is both cosmic and located right in my neighborhood: the church.

If we are Christians, as those who follow Jesus have been called since the first century, our identity is in Christ. And He says to us corporately, as He has since the first century: *Be my church.*

In my travels over the past few years, I've seen what I've known theologically for decades, but the reality is urgent and tangible, and provokes tears in me now. *The local church is God's designed, ordained, and blood-bought instrument of transformation in this dark world.* It is the visible local church in a community—yes, even though it is populated by flawed people like you and me—that shows the world what the invisible Kingdom of God looks like.

Now, just as in His first-century Jesus revolution, God's design is to transform the world through this humble vehicle. In our wonderful Western focus on systems, methods, metrics, and movements, we can sometimes lose sight of God's unlikely plan, which has not changed over the millennia. The local church—peculiar, unglamorous, and imperfect—is God's Plan A for the ages. And, as many Christian leaders have noted, there is no Plan B.

The key to durable hope, refreshment, and joy in these weary times comes not in Big, Fast, New Things but in a what is usually a slow, small thing—the often-unlovely, always-imperfect local church.

And in this, God meets us with a wonderful paradox, for these millions of flawed, small churches are part now of what will one day be fully revealed as the whole enchilada: the magnificent, glorious, cosmic, and enormous whole, the splendor that Jesus Himself started; the capital-C Church. Multicultural, multilingual, multi-abled, multigenerational; hilarious with diversity and yet gloriously solemn in its unity, "spread through all time and space and rooted in eternity, terrible as an army with banners":[a] the mysterious bride of Christ, the glorious community of the beloved.

But not yet.

As we wait for that great day of consummation, God has given us everything we need, wherever we live, to be His people in this ordinary day. We don't need something new and improved. We need to be reminded of what we know to be true and have perhaps cast aside as too tedious or inconvenient.

In this, as always, God is gracious. He loves us. He sees us where we are. And if we have the humility to see as well, the family of God in developing nations around the world can encourage those of us in the weary, wealthier places.

Chapter 3

NOT A RELIGION

Religion says, "I obey; therefore I am accepted."
Christianity says, "I'm accepted, therefore I obey."
Jesus isn't one more teacher, come to tell you how to save yourself and find God.
He is God himself, come to save and find you.

TIMOTHY KELLER,
Gospel In Life Study Guide

Some years ago, I wrote a book with my friend and all-around groovy guy, pastor Greg Laurie. *Jesus Revolution* depicted the wild way in which the Holy Spirit moved in the early 1970s, a tumultuous time of unrest in America and hand-wringing despair among many.

In short, God worked among the least likely people—the drug- and sex-crazed hippies—to begin an awakening which then became revival for churches open enough to welcome people different from their usual parishioners and to participate in the tide of the Holy Spirit.

Well, the book became a movie or, as they say, "a major motion picture." (I live for the day when a book cover bears the banner, "Now a minor motion picture.") *Jesus Revolution* did well at the box office. It lives on, approximately forever, on various streaming services. Aside from the fact that it's fun to write a book that becomes a movie, I don't think what we need today is a *new* Jesus revolution, as that can be so easily misunderstood in these politically volatile times. The Jesus revolution of the early 1970s had staying power precisely because many of its new converts became disciples through the fellowship and teaching of local churches.

Jesus did not come to start a revolution or a movement or a philosophy or even a religion.

The first-century Roman world was full of religions. The more, the merrier. The Greeks, in particular, were always intrigued by cool new philosophies, as if human beings could think their way to enlightenment. Meanwhile, the religions of the day centered around rules, rituals, and sacrifices or other methods to win the favor of often-volatile gods.

But Christianity was, and is, distinct from any religious system, ancient or modern, that teaches people how to find God. It is a relationship with God, initiated by God, who loved us enough to come and find us.

Many of us know this in our heads. I was reminded recently of what it looks like by a bearded guy from Hezbollah.

Omer is in his mid-thirties and looks, perhaps, like Jesus. I met him in Turkey. He grew up in Diyarbakır, on a high plateau on the banks of the Tigris River. His extended family were Sunni Muslims who were Hezbollah radicals in a time when the Turkish government sought to eradicate activist cells.

As a child, Omer received propaganda and guerrilla-fighting training. In 1999, when Omer was about eight, several of his relatives were scooped up in a police raid and never seen again. In 2000, Omer's activist older brother, Umit, was arrested and badly beaten, but he escaped. Omer listened with wonder to his stories about great heroes like Osama bin Laden and the *mujahideen* in Afghanistan. Even as a child, Omer cheered *Allahu Akbar!* on the streets on September 11, 2001.

In 2003, Omer's older brother, Umit, saw an ad in a local newspaper: "Would you like to read *Incil* [the New Testament in Turkish]?"

The ad gave the address of a church. Umit had never read the Bible, but he thought this was a way he could infiltrate a Christian community and lead the infidels back to Islam.

> It is a relationship with God, initiated by God, who loved us enough to come and find us.

Umit told his brothers, "I'm going to see the Christians. If I don't come back, come and rescue me!"

Umit did get rescued, though not in the way he had anticipated. In conversation and questions and answers with the Christians, he ended up surrendering his activist life to Jesus.

"This made an earthquake in our family," Omer says today. "My dad was called upon as a *mullah* [teacher of Islam] in that community, and then his oldest son goes and becomes Christian.

"They didn't kill him, though. 'He's still young,' they said. 'He'll come back to Islam.'

"Then my brother's character and life started changing," Omer continues. "He would spend time helping the younger ones in our family. I went with my brother to the church."

In Sunday school, Omer heard about Jesus, "but I didn't remember anything about Him except He was from Nazareth, born in Bethlehem. What I remember was the love of those people in the church. They loved children and actually paid attention to them.

"At the same time I was going to church, I was going to Hezbollah [youth] gatherings; though I was a child, I would compare them."

Umit left town to perform his compulsory military service, and Omer drifted away from the church, though he never forgot the love there.

Omer's father took him to the leaders of Hezbollah.

"My son is your son," he said. "You can teach him from now on." Over time, Omer studied to be a *muezzin* (the man who calls Muslims to prayer) of the local mosque. He immersed himself in religion, learning *sharia* law, and worked on his Arabic so he could understand the Qur'an, not just recite it. Wearing a white headdress like an Arab, he connected with Hezbollah cells in Lebanon and lost friends who were fighting for Al Qaeda in Syria.

"Every once in a while," he says, "I'd see my brother, who now lived in another town. I was thinking he was so stupid for converting. I thought, 'I need to kill those people who made my brother Christian. According to the Qur'an, my brother should be killed.'"

But Omer couldn't kill his brother.

One day, as they were walking to visit family, Omer burst out to Umit, "Why did you become a Christian? How is that possible?"

"Look," said Umit, pointing to the end of the road. "If someone told me, 'Your death is waiting for you down the street,' I would run toward it. When I was Muslim, I would run the other way."

"Impossible!" shouted Omer. "You've been brainwashed to know you'll have life after death! Even Muhammad was not sure he would be in heaven. Ask any Muslim if he's going to heaven, he'll just say *inshallah* [God willing]."

Omer couldn't get his brother's words out of his mind. After all, the only way in Islam to be sure of paradise was to die in *jihad*. That's why Omer wanted to do it. It was dying for Islam—and you get a bonus. All those virgins!

A few more years went by. Omer's mentorship in Hezbollah

continued, as did both his radical convictions and some nagging questions as he understood more of the Qur'an. A few years later, a cousin came to faith in Jesus. Omer and the cousin got stranded in another city, and a Christian friend of the cousin's paid for their transportation home.

So, Omer was indebted. Courtesy demanded that now he had to go to the church youth meeting to thank the guy. It was the same church community he had visited as a kid with his older brother.

"When I entered the house, everyone was clapping and cheering, 'Ah, Omer!' They remembered me from when I was a child! They knew my story. These people knew I would want to kill them, but they were so happy to see me.

"That meeting was a turning point for me. I had to go again. For one month, I went to just the youth meetings—never to Sunday church. I didn't want Muslims to see me. But I saw the same love I had received as a child. It touched me."

Omer spent an anguished year trying to know what to do. He felt like he would be sinning if he rejected Islam and became an infidel. The *mullahs* visited constantly, trying to convince him to continue in his Islamic studies and religious practices. His father was furious and beat him badly until his mother intervened.

"I wasn't Muslim, and I wasn't a Christian," Omer says. He lied to everyone, went to church and to the mosque. "I prayed, 'Allah, I know you exist, but whose god are you? God of Christians or god of Muslims?'"

There was no single dramatic moment. No nighttime vision. Just a steady, growing sense of the truth, then repentance and a heart that began to change.

Omer's father disowned him, kicked Omer out of the house after making him remove the clothing and shoes that "I bought you, and now you are an infidel," forbade family members to help him, and divorced Omer's mother for allowing him to convert.

Omer had nothing. He went to the church, where Pastor Ahmet, a faithful, mentoring Christian leader in this part of Turkey, took him in. Omer was baptized. He worked cleaning the church, which paid him a small stipend.

He was young, hungry, wearing borrowed clothes, separated from his family, and confused. One day he was praying during the worship service, worrying and wondering what to do with his life. "As I prayed, I felt someone tapping me on the shoulder. I turned around, once, twice, no one was there. I opened my Bible, and suddenly these verses popped out."

Omer had never seen them before. He took them to heart. They gave him the faith to carry on.

> Therefore I tell you, do not be anxious about your life, what you will eat or what you will drink, nor about your body, what you will put on … your heavenly Father knows that you need them all. But seek first the kingdom of God and his righteousness, and all these things will be added to you.[3]

Today Omer is married, has a family, and serves as a deacon in his small church of about 60 people. He's had educational and theological training, and is responsible for discipleship, as well as youth ministry—which pulled him in, years ago—and also evangelistic outreaches. He is also helping with church plants in four other cities.

The spiritual soil in Turkey is hard, but he presses on.

"God is working miraculously," he says. "God is bringing Hezbollah people into the church. We have one guy who came to us from the political arm of Hezbollah. 'I heard about you!' he told me.

"Another young man came to church to harm us. He came

---

3 Matthew 6:25, 32, 33.

for a few months, then disappeared. After a year he came back, completely changed. 'I saw you were so different,' he said. 'I couldn't hurt you. I started to change inside, and now I am a believer!'"

Omer says the church's goals are pretty simple: "We share the gospel with people so they might believe and accept salvation, and we teach them so they will share with others."

Most important, in this Muslim land, "we are teaching that Christianity is not a religion. It's a relationship that lives inside of you."

So, the former revolutionary, former religious zealot, now teaches people about a living relationship with Jesus Christ.

Just like the first-century Christians in the book of Acts.

Chapter 4

THE CHURCH THAT JESUS STARTED

"But what about you?" [Jesus] asked. "Who do you say I am?" Simon Peter answered, "You are the Messiah, the Son of the living God." Jesus replied, "Blessed are you, Simon son of Jonah, for this was not revealed to you by flesh and blood, but by my Father in heaven. And I tell you that you are Peter, and on this rock I will build my church, and the gates of Hades will not overcome it."

MATTHEW 16:15-18, NIV

The church is constituted as a new people who have been gathered from the nations to remind the world that we are in fact one people. Gathering … is the foretaste of the unity of the communion of the saints.

STANLEY HAUERWAS, *In Good Company*

As our brother Omer says, Jesus didn't start a religion. He started a *church.*

Think about early on during Jesus' public ministry, when ordinary people were intrigued by His teaching and gobsmacked by His miracles. One day Jesus asked His followers who the crowds thought He was.[4]

The responses were mixed. A prophet like Elijah, perhaps, or maybe John the Baptist, whom Herod had executed.

Then Jesus asked His closest friends who *they* thought He was.

Poor Simon Peter often missed the point, but he got this answer right: "You are the Messiah, the Son of the living God."[5]

Remember that Jesus, who liked both puns and nicknames, had started calling His friend "Cephas" in Aramaic, which was translated as "Peter" in Greek.[6] Both names in their respective languages sound like the word we know in English as "rock." So, after Peter had gotten something right and declared that Jesus was the Messiah, the Son of the living God, Jesus blessed him. He said that God Himself had revealed this to his rock-like friend.[7]

"And on this rock," Jesus continued, "I will build my church."[8]

It would be an unstoppable force, stronger than the gates of hell.

Whether Jesus meant that He would build His church on Peter himself or upon Peter's confession of faith is a matter that various faith traditions interpret differently. But the point is, the church is not a human enterprise. Jesus Christ is the One who builds it.

But before it could get off the ground, someone had to come: the Holy Spirit.

After Jesus rose from the grave and returned to Heaven—before the Spirit arrived and the church began—Jesus' first followers brimmed with passion and urgency. Jesus had been

---

4 Matthew 16:13-14.
5 Matthew 16:16, NIV.
6 See John 1:42.
7 Matthew 16:17.
8 v 18.

dead, really dead, and now He was alive! He was the promised One, the Savior of the world! He was coming back soon, probably within the next year or so! Time was of the essence!

Jesus had told them their calling: "You will be my witnesses in Jerusalem, and in all Judea and Samaria, and to the end of the earth."[9]

In other words (paraphrasing what my friend and pastor David Platt says), Jesus' charge was basically this.

Go to where they hate you (Jerusalem, where Jesus had just been executed).

Go to people like you (Judea).

Go to people you hate because of traditional ethnic bias (Samaria).

And, oh yes, also go to really faraway places that you don't even know exist, assuming you don't fall off the edge of the world first.

But the disciples could not obey that calling by the power of their own enthusiasm. Jesus had said, "But you will receive power when the Holy Spirit has come upon you."[10] Only then would they be able to be His witnesses.

So, the newly galvanized Jesus followers didn't get to gallop off right away.

Wait, He told them before He went up to Heaven. *Whoa. Do not leave Jerusalem but wait for the gift my Father promised. In a few days you will be baptized with the Holy Spirit.*[11]

So they waited for the Father's gift, whatever that baptism would look like and no matter how strange and frightening it might be. They gathered in Jerusalem, about 120 men and women, devoting themselves to prayer.[12]

And one fine day, the thunderous, fiery wind of the Holy Spirit descended.

---

9 Acts 1:8.

10 v 8.

11 Paraphrased from Acts 1:4-5.

12 Acts 1:14-15.

Outside the open windows of the house, foreign visitors to Jerusalem from Asia, Egypt, Rome, Libya, and Mesopotamia heard—and understood—the tsunami of praise that day. "How is it that we hear," they marveled, "each of us in his own native language … we hear them telling in our own tongues the mighty works of God."[13]

The rest of the book of Acts describes the mind-blowing reality that the good news of Messiah Jesus was not only for the Jews, like those who heard the thunder of the day of Pentecost, *but also for non-Jews.* The gospel was for all the nations, meaning not geographical countries per se but ethnolinguistic groupings of people all over the face of the earth to whom Jesus followers had the responsibility to preach the gospel and make disciples.[14]

> The church is communal, not individual.

The believers knew it was not a human movement. They did not expect the new church to be built through the established structures of political, cultural, military, or religious power. Certainly, people from those arenas experienced the pull of the Holy Spirit and came to faith, but the believers did not look to the kingdoms of this world to advance the Kingdom of God.[15]

So, what did this new thing look like?

When Jesus told Peter He would build His church on the rock, the Greek word Jesus used, *petra,* means a mass of *connected* rock, which is distinct from the similar word that means a detached stone or boulder. This fits, for the church is

13 Acts 2:8, 11.

14 Matthew 28:18-20.

15 Though the disciples had originally thought the Messiah had come to establish a kingdom on earth by banishing Roman political power and setting up a theocracy, after Christ's resurrection, they slowly got the idea.

communal, not individual.

Certainly, God first calls us to Himself as *individuals*. As I've said, Jesus saves us intimately, by the power of the Holy Spirit. We will one day stand before Him on our own.

But Christianity is not a private, individualistic relationship between a person and God. When Christ saves a person, He places him or her in a group. The new life in Christ is, by definition, *corporate*. Jesus calls us out into a new Kingdom community.

Yes, hermits and those in solitary confinement and others in enforced isolation can know Jesus and enjoy intimate fellowship with Him. But the New Testament norm is that faith in Jesus is lived out in connection with others. The Lord's prayer is a corporate prayer. *Our* Father. Give *us* our daily bread. Forgive *us*. Lead *us*. Deliver *us*.

Every New Testament metaphor for the church is communal in its fullness.

The church is known as *the body* of Christ: one body of many parts, each one uniquely fulfilling its purpose, just like our human bodies, so that we build up the whole.[16]

Similarly, the church is *God's household*, made up of members doing various tasks while all holding fast to our common hope in Him.[17]

The church is also called *the temple* of God, built with living stones—us—with Christ as both foundation and cornerstone.[18]

The Greek word Jesus used for church is *ekklesia*.[19] It means the "called out" ones—an assembly of people. It was used in Greek culture to denote a gathering of citizens, as on

16 See Romans 12:4-5; 1 Corinthians 10:17, 12:12, 12:27; Ephesians 4:4-5; Colossians 1:24.

17 See Hebrews 3:6; 1 Timothy 3:14-15; 1 Peter 4:17.

18 See 1 Corinthians 3:11, 16-17; Ephesians 2:19-22; 1 Peter 2:5-6.

19 Also spelled *ecclesia*.

occasions when they convened out of their houses to vote.

In the New Testament, *ekklesia* referred to both the micro and the macro: the word was used for individual local congregations, like my church or your church. This is called the church particular. It was also used for the universal church: all believers worldwide and through history.

For the purposes of this book, focus for just a moment on those terms.[20]

The Church Universal

I grew up hearing missionary stories. My family was part of a missions-focused denomination, and my parents practiced the gift of hospitality. Whenever missionaries were on furlough in the US, visiting various churches that supported them financially, they would stay at our house. They'd pull out the tech of the day—their Kodak photos and their little cardboard-bordered celluloid images shown on their handy slide projectors. They'd tell about people who had never heard about Jesus, and how they had responded to the good news about His love for everyone. They talked about families giving up their household idols, being baptized in their new church communities, learning how to read the Bible in their own languages, and reaching out to others as their churches grew.

Those rich dinner-table stories weren't just stand-alone, self-contained episodes of exotic locales and faraway happenings. Their power lay in the fact that I knew I was *connected* to these people in Vietnam or India or South America. Though the people in their stories spoke different languages than I did and ate different foods and lived in different types of houses than my suburban rambler, we were connected.

---

20 These points are fleshed out far more fully in a book called *Being the Body*, which I wrote with my mentor and friend Chuck Colson more than 25 years ago.

I was a kid, but I got it. In my mind, the missionaries sitting at my family's dining room table might as well have been Paul or Barnabas or some first-century Christians who had traveled to faraway lands and were now reporting back on what God had done in those places. The faraway people that the missionaries talked about were my brothers and sisters in Christ, just like the people in Acts. We were part of the same family. And when I worshiped God in my little church outside of Washington, DC on Sunday mornings, I was part of something so much bigger.

As I got older, my theology got fancier, but the main points were the same. I knew from the Bible that I was connected to the great "cloud of witnesses"—all the believers throughout time who had preceded me.[21] I was also connected to all the Christ followers alive today, all over the world. This church universal is an invisible superstructure that spans the world as well as the centuries of human existence. It's a house or a castle or a palace not built with human hands but by the Spirit of God Himself.

The church universal is the great fellowship of all throughout eternal history who have been redeemed by the blood of Jesus. We will not all be physically together until God establishes His "new heaven and new earth."[22] The church universal is the Bride for which Jesus will one day return—the people from every tribe and nation who will one day worship around His throne in Heaven. In that great day, there will be no more individual, particular churches. Just the glorious ultimate body of Christ—the people bought by His blood, whose names are written in His book.

It is a good thing to hold this cosmic vision of Jesus' big-C Church in our minds. Every Christ follower is part of the

---

21 Hebrews 12:1.

22 Revelation 21:1.

same church universal. It's invisible right now, and we will not see it in its fullness until we stand in eternity.

The Church Particular

For now, we deal in the realm of the church particular. Your local church. My local church. The gatherings of Christ-followers in various places around the globe, whether they meet under a mango tree in Africa, in a village prayer house in India, or in a megachurch in Albuquerque. One hesitates to list its identifying characteristics; some renowned pastors say there are nine marks of the church, others say twelve or six or four.

I'm not a theologian expositing the book of Acts or the rest of the New Testament. But certainly, we can see common characteristics of the local *ekklesia*. The early believers were devoted to Scripture and devoted to one other. They ate meals together, particularly obeying Jesus' sacramental instructions in His Last Supper before His death and resurrection. They were devoted to prayer, unity, and generosity for those in need. They shared the good news and baptized and mentored new believers. They were joyful and full of awe—because, in all of this, they were filled with the non-human, supernatural presence of the Holy Spirit.

The early believers were devoted to Scripture and devoted to one other.

Again, they weren't devotees practicing some new religion; they were transformed people living out the reign of King Jesus on this broken earth: a hint of what will one day be realized in its fullness. As J.I. Packer wrote years ago, echoing John Calvin, "The task of the church is to make the invisible Kingdom visible" in every ordinary sphere of human life and need.[b]

Whether in first-century Palestine or modern-day Brazil, Botswana, Buffalo, or Bangladesh, this is the pattern of God's new community. People come together to worship, pray, learn, eat, share, take the sacraments, be held accountable, and walk with one another in the joys and messes of everyday life. Then they go out to share their overflow of God's grace with outsiders.

And it is the unity of the local church that shows the world that Jesus is the Son of God. He prayed, "… that they may all be one, just as you, Father, are in me, and I in you, that they also may be in us, so that the world may believe that you have sent me … and loved them even as you loved me."[23]

This oneness is not based on the local church being made up of people who share the same background, education, ethnicity, inclinations, and opinions. The world has those. They're called clubs. The church is different. Its unity of disparate personalities and preferences testifies to the supernatural power of God.

C.S. Lewis wrote that…

> … the Church is not a human society of people united by their natural affinities but the Body of Christ, in which all members, however different (and He rejoices in their differences and by no means wishes to iron them out) must share the common life, complementing and helping one another precisely by their differences.[c]

To happily summarize for our purposes going forward, every Christ follower is part of the same church universal. It's

23 John 17:21, 23.

invisible right now, and we will not see it in its fullness until we stand in eternity.

And in our lives here on earth, we are called to become part of local, particular congregations. These churches are humble, imperfect, full of flawed human beings, just like in the book of Acts. But it is the local *ekklesia* that God has called to show the world what the Kingdom of Heaven looks like. As the church is a beacon of love, joy, truth, worship, peace, and unity, it foretells what the Kingdom will be like in its ultimate fulfillment.

This was God's plan, to be carried out by ordinary human beings but built by Christ Himself and fueled by the Holy Spirit.

It's the church that Jesus started, made up of the people called by His name. It is irrepressible, a forever family woven together of people from every tribe and nation—people who dwell in the various nation-states of this world but whose highest and eternal allegiance is to the Kingdom of God.

I've had the opportunity to visit many book-of-Acts-type churches. So, like those missionaries who sat at my parents' dining room table so many decades ago, I need to tell the stories of ordinary Jesus followers in these churches around the world, and the secret to their durable faith.

I've included only a handful of the tremendous stories I gathered during my travels. But the ones in this book show some important characteristics of the early church. Not didactically but through the power of story. And please bear in mind: some of these stories may be from denominations or traditions you're not familiar with or even feel a bit uncomfortable with. But all of them are from churches that cleave to the fundamentals that have distinguished real Christianity since its beginnings.

So, what good can the church, lived out from its ancient model, do for real 21st-century people in desperate situations?

Chapter 5

THE COMMUNITY THAT HELPS THE DESPERATE

We work out our faith with these other broken men and women around us in the pews. It's lackluster. It can be boring or taxing. It's often messy. It's sometimes painful. But these Christians around me become each other's call and response. We remind each other of the good news. All saints and sinners in the church share together in this gospel. The meal would be incomplete if even one of these was not at the table.

TISH HARRISON WARREN,
Liturgy of the Ordinary

If there was ever a person who seemed like she was destined to a life of hopeless isolation and death by her own hand, it was my Russian sister Tatiana. But instead, she's now living a life of flourishing hope—because the church is a community that welcomes the desperate and broken.

All that Tatiana can remember, all these years later, is a flash of light in the dark rain and a bump, and then she was ejected onto the wet street. There was the explosive clash of a second crash, and all went dark.

She had been in the right front passenger seat of a small,

Soviet-era two-door car. The man she lived with was driving; her young daughter and a woman who needed a ride were in the back. When another vehicle hit their small car, and then a second car skidded and hit them as well, all three died.

Tatiana, a Russian living in Tajikistan, was taken to the hospital in her town, a gaping wound in her head and her body broken. The staff didn't expect her to survive. Doctors did what they could and put her in a waiting area while they tended other patients.

An old lady wrapped in a headscarf stopped at her bed. "I'm here to visit those who are left here to die," she told Tatiana in Russian.

This was less than encouraging.

The woman went on. "I'm here to talk to you about God. You need to thank Him—you could be dead. He has given you a second chance to thank Him, and live."

Tatiana could not even respond to the *babushka*. She was so angry. Why would anyone thank God? It was His fault that her body was crushed, that her young daughter had died. And her partner? He was a strong man—much stronger than she was! Why would he die? And the woman they had given a ride to? She had four children, the youngest just a baby. Why would God take her?

Impossibly, Tatiana got stronger. She learned to walk again. She was released from the hospital. She moved to a different town. She abused alcohol to cope. She drank all the time, somehow functioning at her job, but nothing eased her pain and anger. At night she hung with new friends—people who knew she had money and needed booze as much as she did.

One night, a woman at the bar offended Tatiana. This was not hard to do. Tatiana cursed at her, the argument escalated, and in the haze of cigarette smoke, clanging beer bottles, and a crowd of drunken men, Tatiana knocked the woman to the floor. She got her strong hands around the woman's neck, squeezed, and didn't let go. By the time the chaos stilled and the room stopped spinning, the woman was limp on the dirty floor. Dead.

Tatiana was sentenced to ten years in a prison in the north of Tajikistan.

The prison was full of tough women, but the inmates still gave Tatiana space. It was obvious she was desperate and could blow at any time, and it would be violent. Meanwhile, her mind wore thin with the same circuitous thoughts. *Why? Why did my daughter die in the car crash and I did not? Where was God?*

One afternoon Tatiana's cellmate said, "We should go to the prayer room; they're having a meeting of the Baptists."

All Tatiana could think was how much she wanted to beat up her fellow inmate for suggesting such a thing. Everyone knew that Baptists were cannibals who ate people and drank their blood.

"Come on," said the other woman, oblivious that her intact facial features were hanging by a thread. "They'll serve bread and tea."

Tea! Tatiana had been longing for tea. When her mother had visited and neglected to bring her packets of tea, Tatiana had cursed her out.

"You go," she said sullenly.

Later, though, Tatiana made her way to the prayer room. A man was preaching. The people seemed normal; they were smiling. And there was bread and tea and other snacks.

Tatiana kept coming back. For six months she listened to the Bible teaching. She realized that the Baptists were not only not cannibals but also friendly and faithful. They also kept coming back, week after week. Tatiana understood from them that Jesus was the Savior and loves everyone… but she concluded that what she had done could not be forgiven.

Finally, one of the church volunteers sat down with her.

"Every week I see you are listening," she said. "You answer questions—but there is no light in your eyes."

It was Tatiana's birthday, March 16. She felt nostalgic. She told the woman her story… and the woman opened the Gospel of Luke to the story of the man on the cross next to Christ's, the one who had committed terrible crimes, but was promised paradise.[24]

Tatiana saw scenes from her life, like the times she was drunk and had beaten up her mother or the occasion when she assaulted a pregnant lady because she wasn't polite. She couldn't cry. She had a stone in her throat. She remembered the *babushka* who had said God kept her alive for a chance to live.

A few words tumbled out. "God, if You really exist, if You can really forgive me like You forgave that man on the cross next to Christ, please forgive me!"

Somehow Tatiana calmed down. She went back to her bunk in her cell. She slept.

The next morning, she woke early. She went out to the prison yard. There were the same high walls, the same barbed wire, the rough shouts of the guards for morning roll call. But Tatiana had never seen the skies so beautiful. There were some little red tulips in a planter, and now, as the sun touched them, they opened toward the sky.

Tatiana stopped breathing.

"Oh, God, what You have made! This is so beautiful!"

Tatiana got in formation, but that day she held her head up. She actually looked at the other women. One, she knew, had no idea where her children were—and Tatiana felt something for her. It was compassion. Unprecedented. The mother of another inmate had had a heart attack, and the woman had been so worried. Tatiana had scoffed before, but now she felt empathy.

---

24 Luke 23:39-43.

"These women!" she thought. "They need hope. They need God."

But there was a problem. "I can't tell them about Him. I have no words. Only curse words. I have nothing but bad words."

Tatiana didn't know what to do.

So, she did not speak for three days.

And then a teenaged inmate moved Tatiana's cup a fraction of an inch during a meal. Tatiana exploded with three days of suppressed rage and filth.

The girl was a tough character. But she fled, in tears.

Tatiana went to the prayer room and cried, "God, what do I do? I have no words!"

Her eyes fell on the big bookshelf the Baptists had stocked with Bibles and Christian literature. Ah. Maybe she could soak her mind in *God's* words, and He would take care of the problem.

She did, and He did.

After four more years in prison as part of the church behind the barbed wire, Tatiana was released. Her Baptist brothers and sisters were waiting for her at the prison gate, and she traveled with them to Tajikistan's capital, Dushanbe. She planted herself in the Prayer House for All Nations there. The believers welcomed her; she continued to grow in faith and wisdom.

And then, in 2017 an opportunity opened that seemed both crazy and perfect for Tatiana. A brother from the church had started a ministry to homeless women and children, and now local Christians had found a property to refurbish and establish the home on a more official basis. The church leaders asked Tatiana if she would become the director.

Tatiana could not believe it. She prayed. She accepted the job. On her first day, she looked at the faces of the women looking up at her, their children on their laps. They seemed like little, lost sheep. No hope. Nowhere to go. She knew how they felt.

Tatiana hasn't counted all the women and children she has helped over the years. Some women live at the Hope Center for weeks until they can get on their feet and connect with relatives or jobs elsewhere. Some stay for a long time. Some children are brought alone, like Asiya. When she was brought to the center, she was a toddler with a big head and curved limbs like skinny sticks. She couldn't walk, feed herself, or talk. Whenever she saw a man, she would whimper in fear.

Volunteers from the church helped Tatiana massage Asiya's little limbs. They patiently taught her how to eat with forks and spoons. They read her Bible stories and prayed that she would learn to talk.

> Her story shows how God uses a local body of believers, that the life with Christ is not meant to be lived alone, that the church must be a community that reaches out together to the broken.

If you visit Tatiana today, you'll see Asiya. Now she wears a plaid jumper and a tiara in her thick, curly hair. She's healthy, curious, active, and, in Tatiana's words, "never stops talking."

And in Tatiana you will find a peaceful person who lives the love of Jesus for women and children who seem beyond hope. She will tell you, "If you knew me before, you would see I am a miracle of God. During my first three years in prison, I tried to commit suicide. I tried to hang myself. Four different times. All I wanted was to die.

"But God protected my life. Now I see His task for me. I want to live. And I live to do His work."

Tatiana's unlikely story shows God's transforming power. Only He can bring a dead soul to new life. Her story also shows how God uses a local body of believers, that the life with Christ is not meant to be lived alone, that the church must be a community that reaches out together to the broken.

Without the Christ followers who came so faithfully into her prison, Tatiana likely wouldn't have heard the gospel. Without their perseverance—they just kept coming back—she wouldn't have responded. Without their discipleship in the Scriptures, she wouldn't have grown. Without their help after she was released from prison, she wouldn't have made it to her new church community. And without that church, she wouldn't have continued growing steadily in her faith and finding the fruitful, enduring ministry for which God designed her, a ministry that touches desperate lives, child by child, woman by woman, for eternal change.

Chapter 6

THE ULTIMATE HALF-TIME GUY

There is not a square inch in the whole domain of our human existence over which Christ, who is Sovereign over all, does not cry, "Mine!"

ABRAHAM KUYPER, Address at the Inauguration of the Free University

You can get a lot done if you don't care who gets the credit.

DR. RALPH WINTER

So, you may or may not wonder, how is it that I could just climb on random airplanes and interview Jesus people like Tatiana in Tajikistan and other faraway places? (Regarding my travels, some have asked did I actually eat that furry boiled monkey in the Amazon jungle? What about, in other places, the deep-fried rodent or the special fatty lamb tail or the unidentified deceased-mammal stew, or "Smiley," the boiled sheep's head that is a popular street food in South Africa? The answer is that I am sadly narrow in my preferences and become an ardent vegetarian whenever I leave the US. But I digress.)

My connection with all this is International Cooperating Ministries, or ICM, the ministry that works with Paul

Hagelgans, whom we met in chapter 1, and 300 vibrant Jesus-loving partners like him around the world.

This book began, on a whiteboard, as a history of ICM. Then we all realized that the topic was much bigger than one particular ministry. But let me tell you very briefly about ICM, as its mission illuminates our big-picture focus on the church that Jesus started.

ICM comes alongside indigenous Christian leaders in about 100 nations. It partners with local ministries in countries from Albania to Zambia to build churches and equip believers with solid biblical discipleship materials.

I first connected with ICM in 2000.

I had already known Dois Rosser, its founder, because he was a good friend of Chuck Colson, with whom I worked for 20 years. I knew Dois to be a tall, courtly Virginia businessman who loved God and wanted to further His Kingdom.

What I didn't know was that Dois was a wild man for Jesus. I didn't know that he'd started a little parachurch organization and that ICM would turn my life upside down.

Dois called me out of the blue one summer evening in 2000 to see if I'd be interested in writing a book with and for him about what God was doing through the ministry.

"I don't know," I told him. "I'd need to see the ministry in action, on the ground."

Dois Rosser never wasted time. Two weeks later I found myself in southeast Asia, traveling with Dois and a merry band of brothers and sisters. We went to China, Vietnam, and Cambodia, where ICM had been building church-orphanages to equip local communities of Jesus followers and provide places of refuge for vulnerable children to live and grow in the love of Christ.

One day we were scheduled to go from Cambodia's capital, Phnom Penh, to the country's northwestern rural interior to visit pastors and partners. But unusually heavy rains had washed out the roads. Ever the entrepreneur, Dois had somehow arranged for us to rise above this challenge by leasing alternative transportation.

As we arrived at a small military airport to catch our ride, we noted an ancient helicopter on the tarmac. Its rotors were bent, its tires were flat. It looked like a mammoth, smashed insect. How quaint, I thought. This must be a museum for antique aircraft.

But no. This was our ride: a Soviet-era, no, actually a primeval Russian helicopter.

Dois strode cheerfully toward the rusty insect. Compelled by his enthusiasm, the rest of our group dutifully climbed up a rickety ladder and into the belly of the beast. The seams of the fuselage didn't quite meet; we could see blue sky through the gaps. An enormous yellow fuel tank, plastered with a "No Smoking" warning in Russian, took up most of the space in the "cabin." (I had not been thinking of lighting up just then.)

Our seats were white plastic lawn chairs scattered about for our traveling comfort. Through the cockpit door, I could see that one of the pilots was sitting on an upended wooden box. No tray tables in the upright and locked position; no flight attendants pointing out the exits and the inflatable rafts in the "unlikely event of a water landing." No, when we crashed, we would just climb out one of the open portholes, should we still be alive to do so.

It was clear we were all going to die.

We prayed. The ancient engines sputtered to life. The propellers spun. The yellow fuel tank jiggled. The helicopter shuddered, shook, and then pitched forward like a drunk person running for the restroom.

And then we were somehow aloft, skimming above the jungle green and the flooded rice paddies, alive and well over God's good earth. Flooded with the exhilaration of actually being alive, I was overwhelmed by everything I saw and heard about ICM's work in Cambodia—and then Vietnam and China—for the rest of that trip.

I tell this story not out of some twisted desire that its absurdity might make you smile but because it shows so clearly the inexorably creative, urgent, committed, and faith-filled personality of this role model who so affected my life. Dois Rosser would not be stopped. He *had* to get to the ministry partners, flood or no flood. He could not let them down.

To this day, Dois's urgency and humble love for the worldwide body of Christ have energized me.

So has the story that we heard on that long-ago trip, the story of the God who hung on the cross that I told at the beginning of this book. Think of that remote Cambodian village, back in the 1970s, waiting for the gospel. They knew of something more than ancestor worship and animistic traditions. They had heard just a whisper about Jesus… but they'd been waiting for the rest of the story. Just like Gulshamal, the blind woman with leprosy in Kazakhstan, waiting for the same gospel. And now, in both those places, ICM-built churches reach out to the local communities.

As our helicopter adventure made clear to me, Dois Rosser was a man propelled by an inner urgency to reach the world, the whole world, for Christ. He'd exploit any kind of technology, any resource, to do so. And his story is a great model of lavishly pouring out his life and resources in the service of God.

Decades ago, Dois was leading a lovely American-dream-type life. He was a successful entrepreneur who had started multiple lucrative businesses and mentored dozens of people over the decades. He and his wife, Shirley, were deeply involved in their local church in Hampton, Virginia, and gave generously to lots of great ministries.

But when Dois stopped long enough in his busy days to think about it, he felt like he had an imaginary dividing line in his life. On one side of the line were "secular" things, like his businesses and community work. On the other side were the things that were "sacred": Christian ministry, church commitments, missionary support.

Even as he began to reflect on this neat division, Dois's spiritual journey shifted into a higher gear through the teachings of an unlikely pastor. Dick Woodward was a medium-sized guy with medium-brown hair, medium-brown eyes, and a medium-brown voice. He was the pastor of a church in Dois's area, and in spite of his unremarkable appearance, he was drawing 350 local businesspeople every week to a Thursday morning Bible study.

Dois had read the Bible all his life, but he'd never heard it taught in street language, verse by verse, in ways that applied practically and powerfully to daily life.

A few years into his friendship with Dick and his newfound appetite for the Scriptures, Dois sat down one morning with a cup of coffee and a yellow legal pad. He felt like he was at what writer Bob Buford calls a "half-time" moment. He had achieved business success. But what of the second half of life? How could he develop a life of more significance? Dois knew what he believed, spiritually, but what was he going to do with it?

"I had achieved many successes in the first half of the game, so to speak, but I needed to reevaluate," Dois said. "What was really important? How could I use my time, money, and abilities for things that would, in fact, last *forever*?"

He drew a vertical line down the middle of the yellow pad to make two columns and wrote his habitual headings of "Kingdom business" and "secular business." He started listing the various things he was doing and slotting them into one side or the other in his usual division between the sacred and the secular.

And then, it hit him, as if God was saying to him, *Don't you realize that it's one and the same? Your life—all of it—is under My dominion. It's all for My glory.*

Dois had always assumed that his role as a businessman was to make enough money to give generously to Christian outreaches and to fund people in fulltime Christian service. Now he realized that he was a full-time minister of the gospel himself—in the business world. God had called and equipped him specifically to do Kingdom work in every aspect of his life.

Around the same time that God smacked Dois with this epiphany and Dois stopped drawing vertical dividing lines on his legal pads, another ministry-shaping event took place.

As God would have it, in 1986 Dois visited India with an old friend. That's where his appetite for building physical churches began.

Hosted by local Christian leaders, Dois bumped over dusty roads to remote, thatched-hut villages where gaunt women draped in saris cooked rice over cow-dung fires. Dois saw, smelled, and felt the effects of poverty, disease, and sex trafficking, and the dark control of animism, idol worship, and witch doctors.

He also saw the love and power of the Indian believers. He saw how when a church was planted in a village, it transformed the community with the light and the love of Christ. Just like in the book of Acts. And Dois discovered that, at that time, you could build a small, solid church building in India for less than 10,000 dollars.

"What a deal!" he thought.

Dois caucused with Indian believers about where there was already a committed core congregation of local Christians, who just needed a safe, permanent building in which to gather securely. Dois put up the money. The Indians provided the land, did most of the construction themselves, and named their new building the Rosser Memorial Baptist Church. Was

Dois Baptist? No. Was the church Baptist? No. But that's what the Indians wanted to call it.

I visited the Rosser Memorial Baptist Church in 2023, almost 40 years after it had been built. It was a Saturday, with the streets full of shoppers, golden statues and shrines, women in orange and pink saris selling vegetables, motorbikes, and a young man on a bicycle somehow carrying ten trussed live chickens.

> God called and equipped him specifically to do Kingdom work in every aspect of his life.

The church was also full. . . of teenagers. It was holding a conference for young people gathering for intensive Bible teaching and fellowship, which is of course precious to them all in this Hindu-majority nation. The church, over the years, has also planted dozens of daughter churches.

Back to our story from the mid-1980s.

When Dois had first arrived in India, he felt like we all do when we're confronted with mind-boggling human need. Millions and millions of people, entrenched in spiritual slavery to man-made gods. It's overwhelming—what can any of us do in the face of such an immense challenge?

But as Dois started building modest church buildings like the Rosser Memorial Baptist Church for small flocks of Jesus followers, he saw the churches grow as the members grew in grace, shared the gospel, baptized new believers, and reached out to do works of mercy and service in their communities. Then they planted daughter churches to do the same.

Dois felt new hope and excitement. Just as in the first century, when Christ started His church, change most often happens in small ways. One by one by one, the Spirit touches human lives and transforms them; each one passes the gospel on to others, and the body of Christ grows.

Dois got pushback from fellow believers in the US. *Why build churches? The church is not bricks and mortar; it's people!*

Of course. But Dois had seen that in developing countries, the presence of a church building announces to the community that the Christians are here to stay. It shows villagers the beauty, intelligent design, and permanence of God. It serves as a safe house for women and children who are abused. It defrays the suspicion that Christianity is just a Western religion. It provides a place for people to come, raise their children, and grow over time,

And in urban centers, a visible, set-aside church structure can reassure jittery secular authorities.

Consider countries like Turkey and Tajikistan: Muslim-majority with secular constitutions, yet a strong cultural Muslim bias, as well as threats against Christians from radicals.

So, some Western Christians might wonder, why don't the believers just gather in house churches?

First, houses and apartments are typically small and tightly packed. Neighbors complain about singing, tambourines, and too many visitors.

But more significantly, both Turkey and Tajikistan are vigilant about Muslim extremists who seek to subvert the existing government to create an Islamic theocracy. So government officials are suspicious of groups that meet in homes; they could be subversives. But if the crazy Christians build a church and are enthusiastically, openly worshiping God in it, then officials know what they're up to. It's out in the open. (I worshiped in one church in Turkey where the pastor, who'd received death threats from Islamic radicals, is guarded by Muslim policemen provided by the government. Filled with new, young believers, the church is growing steadily.)

Back to Dois.

As the months went by, God led Dois, step by improbable

step. Then—you guessed it—he sat down at his kitchen table with an even larger yellow pad and a bigger cup of coffee. He took stock. He was 65 years old. His real estate and car companies were going very well. He was materially blessed.

And now what?

God had highlighted two essentials for Dois: the priority of durable, secure church buildings and the necessity for sound, biblical discipleship resources to equip both the leadership and the members. God had shown him the church-building component in India and the discipleship component through Dick Woodward's transformational Bible teaching.

Dois sketched lots of ideas on his yellow pad. At a time when most of his colleagues were retiring to play golf every day and sip drinks every evening at the country club, Dois knew God was calling him to start an international ministry.

Not a North American missions agency—no, a cooperating entity that could come alongside indigenous partners, like in India, and equip *their* existing ministry with the resources they needed to catch fire. And because of Dois's business acumen, he knew how to leverage funds that would come from the US to give maximum lift to brothers and sisters in less privileged places.

So in 1986, Dois founded International Cooperating Ministries. The name said it all.

From its small beginnings, God constantly connected ICM with new partners in surprising places. Today it is active in 104 countries, including many I can't name due to security reasons.

For his part, Dois Rosser kept smiling, pushing forward, and inexorably going where God led, climbing onto unsafe travel conveyances all over the world to build new relationships to further the Kingdom of God. He went into the ministry office every day well into his nineties. Then he flew off to Heaven in 2019 at the tender age of 98.

Dois was a father figure to me. I served on his board of directors for many years. Janice Rosser Allen, ICM's president and CEO, is one of my closest friends. I love the ministry's partners and the men and women on its staff.

But again, this is not a book about a particular ministry but about what it stands for: a simple yet profound understanding of *God's* design and plan for the healthy local church, replicated around the world.

And that's what this book is all about.

Chapter 7

THE ELECTRIC CHURCH

Miracles are a retelling in small letters of the very same story which is written across the whole world in letters too large for some of us to see.

C.S. LEWIS, *God in the Dock*

As we consider the church around the world, it's so important to remember *we're* not the ones building it. Again, Jesus is the One doing that.

And what that means, which some of us in the West can sometimes forget, is that He often uses miracles to do so.

C.S. Lewis said that one of the things that led him to believe Christianity was true was that it was unexpected.

> Reality, in fact, is usually something you could not have guessed. That is one of the reasons I believe Christianity. It is a religion that you could not have guessed. If it offered us just the kind of universe we had always expected, I should feel we were making it up. But, in fact, it is not the sort of thing anyone would have made up. It has just that [strange] twist about it that real things have.[d]

It's so true. You can't make this stuff up.

One of my favorite stories—precisely because it is so odd

and supernatural and winsome—comes from the account of the early church in the book of Acts, which overflows with the electric presence and miracles of the Holy Spirit.

There's the main character, Philip. He's evidently Greek, a gifted preacher, and one of the seven men chosen by the early church to specifically care for the poor. God then sends him on a strange special mission to someone in a position of power and influence.[25]

Perhaps Philip was asleep when he got the summons. This happened frequently in the New Testament. Think of Peter, asleep in prison, and an angel woke him up and walked him right out of jail. Or Joseph, Jesus' earthly father, woken in the night and told to take his family and flee to Egypt.

So, we have an angel telling Philip, "Rise!" He was told to go south from Jerusalem to Gaza, a roughly 50-mile trip.

Philip popped up, presumably packed a skin of water and a small bag, and started walking the long desert road.

Eventually he came upon an official entourage that probably had at least one chariot, servants palm-leaf-fanning an important person, baggage carriers, tent-erectors, and others whose job was to make comfortable a court official from what was then called Kush. (Today it's the northern region of Sudan, Egypt's upper Nile, and other areas south of the Sahara.)[c] The official was a eunuch in the service of "Candace," which in Greek was *Kandake*, a female ruler in that region.

Perhaps the chariot had stopped for a moment, so when the Holy Spirit told Philip to join it, he was able to do so. The official was seated, reading a scroll out loud.

Philip recognized the words of the Old Testament prophet Isaiah.

Do you understand it? asked Philip. He knew that Isaiah could be a tough go.

---

25 Acts 8:26-40.

"How can I?" responded the official. There was no one to explain it to him. Except Philip, whom the Holy Spirit had sent.

The official invited Philip to hop in, and as the chariot rolled onward, Philip explained to him that he was reading in Isaiah about Jesus of Nazareth, foretold about 700 years before His birth. He told the guy all about the good news. The man got it, accepted it, and was ready for the next step.

By now the chariot was nearing an oasis.

"Here is water!" said the man. "What prevents me from being baptized?"

The Bible says they both went down into the water, perhaps Philip dunked the official, "and when they came up out of the water, the Spirit of the Lord carried Philip away."

> The early Jesus followers understood that the Spirit of God works in extra-terrestrial ways.

The man from Kush went on his own way, startled by Philip's quick exit but "rejoicing," and most likely carried the good news to his colleagues at home.[26]

So, the Ethiopian guy went joyfully on his way. Philip, meanwhile, teleported about 30 miles. As the Bible understatedly describes it, "Philip found himself at Azotus," or modern-day Ashdod. Philip dusted himself off, found some locals, and went right on preaching.

---

26 It's interesting that the official was a eunuch, which was common in royal courts of the day. Hebrew law, as set out in Deuteronomy, would have excluded anyone who'd been castrated from temple worship. He was reading Isaiah, and just a few chapters after the description of the suffering Jesus in Isaiah 53, Isaiah 56 foretold inclusion for eunuchs and foreigners, among others, in the community of God's people. In Jesus, the prophecies that God's family was for everyone who "holds fast to my covenant" had come true.

What I love about the book of Acts is how such accounts are told so routinely. The early Jesus followers understood that the Spirit of God works in extra-terrestrial ways.

Think of Saul of Tarsus in Acts 9. When he was on his way to Damascus to arrest Christians, a light brighter than the sun knocked him to the ground. In that brilliance too powerful to gaze upon was Jesus, who told Saul that persecuting His people was the same thing as oppressing Him.

As we know, Saul was blinded by the light, humbled, and repentant. Several days later, a brave brother named Ananias put his hands on Saul for him to be healed, by Jesus' power.

Certainly, the mere light of the sun can blind, overwhelming the retina and damaging the optic nerve. Some commentators have suggested that Saul was hit by a bolt of lightning, which can also cause temporary or permanent blindness. And when Ananias prayed for Saul, perhaps the "scales" that fell from his eyes were not just metaphors for his earlier unbelief but actual scabs from the optical injury.

At any rate, I thought of these wild stories from the days of the early church when I sat down with a brother named Yashar. No, he didn't beam from one place to another, like Philip, nor was he temporarily blinded by the Light, like Saul who was renamed Paul.

But God did electrocute him to get his attention.

I met this Pastor Yashar, an enthusiastic man in his mid-sixties, near the ancient site of Antioch in a church distribution center for people in need. The Muslim call to prayer echoed over us from the nearby mosque as we sipped strong, sweet tea, and he told me about his journey to faith.

Born in a small Turkish village, Yashar had a difficult childhood. His dad was ill and couldn't work. From age eight Yashar could not attend school but sold bread on the streets, picked cotton in the fields, and grew bitter because life was so hard. He hated God. When he got older, he joined a socialist group. Eventually he got a job at a textile factory through a communist friend, whom the police later arrested.

Someone gave Yashar's sister a copy of the Bible. She didn't want it and gave it to Yashar. He was curious, as it had been mentioned in passing by some of his socialist colleagues. But he was still angry with God.

By now he was a supervisor at the textile factory and had a separate room there where he often slept. One night he was alone there, reading Jeremiah 29:11-14. The phrases echoed inside of him.

I know the plans I have for you.

For a future and a hope.

When you search for Me, you'll find me.

I will gather you from all the nations.

And as he read each phrase, he heard his name.

"Yashar!"

He started trembling. Terrified. The book fell from his hands.

"It was a fight inside me," he says. "Part of me believed, 'Yes, this is God.' The other part said, 'No, something is wrong with my mind.'

"Okay," said the divided Yashar. "God, if You really exist, I want to know You."

Some nights later, Yashar was reading the dangerous Bible again, now in the New Testament.

"I came to John 11. Verse 35. 'Jesus wept.'

"I started crying. Again, there was a fight in my heart and my mind. I saw *Īsā*—Jesus—as a political hero, close to those who are crying and oppressed. But my mind was saying 'Doesn't *Īsā* have anything better to do other than come to Lazarus's grave and cry in front of all those people?'"

The next morning, Yashar had to get up early. The factory had purchased some updated machinery to be dedicated that day. Management had told him they were bringing in two sheep for the occasion—they would sacrifice them and smear their blood on the new equipment so it would work well.

There was quite a crowd assembled when the bosses told Yashar to commence the big moment and plug in the new machine's huge power cable. Three months earlier, Yashar had taken care to turn off the electrical power at the box when he and his workers removed the old equipment.

He picked up the fat cable from the ground.

"Electricity started flowing through me. I started shaking, I felt like I was dying, quaking in a lightning storm. The heat hit me, it struck the cable out of my hands and into the machine. The machinery started burning. Everybody scattered and ran out of the area.

"I am shaking, looking at the light, shaking and crying, looking at the light. I hear myself cry, *'Īsā!'* It was like He was crying for me there."

Yashar's bosses cut the power. They ran to him. They examined his hands, his feet. No marks. They had a car brought to take him to the hospital.

"No," sobbed Yashar, weeping. He ran to his room, slammed the door, and fell to his knees.

"Īsā!" he cried. "I thank You; I now understand You were crying for me as well! I was against You, but please forgive me. I want You to be the boss of my life."

"Suddenly I felt this strength in my body. I left my room, took a hose, and sprayed water on myself to wash my face, and there in the droplets was a rainbow."

"Let's get you to the hospital!" shouted the bosses.

"No," said Yashar. "I am very well."

There's a postscript from that long-ago day.

As Yashar tells it, "Later, the ladies at the factory were laughing when they saw me.

"'What's so funny?' I asked.

"'Before,' they said, 'whenever you came onto the factory floor, you never smiled or talked, you were angry, everyone tried to avoid you. Since the electricity struck you, you probably just have problems in your head, but you're so much more pleasant!'"

Yashar took it well. He knew Christ had transformed him.

So, he says, "I told them, 'Jesus can change you as well!'

"They said, 'Who is Jesus?'"

And ever since, in his particular part of Turkey, that's the question Yashar has given his life to answer.

Chapter 8

MINARETS OR CROSSES? THE CHURCH THAT ADVANCES

There is no neutral ground in the universe.
Every square inch, every split second, is claimed by God,
and counterclaimed by Satan.

C.S. LEWIS, *The Weight of Glory and Other Essays*

Powered by the holy electricity and power of the Holy Spirit, the early church in the New Testament was not a model of cozy communities who went on retreats. It was a model of the unstoppable advance of the gospel of Jesus. Christians were persecuted, scattered, yet were constantly moving forward to spread the truth about Jesus Christ. They came up against foes and obstacles of every kind. And they kept going, planting new churches of Jesus followers wherever they went.

I've seen the same spirit among church leaders in Tanzania, as they deal with daunting challenges.

Certainly, people in Africa have experienced an explosion of Christian faith over the last few decades. But some of that experience has not been biblically rooted, leading to a prosperity theology that can't go very deep or far.

And there is a massive threat at hand: the orchestrated, well-funded, and aggressive march of Islam. Entrenched in the countries of north Africa, Islam is tactically spreading south, with new mosques being built in towns that don't even have Muslim inhabitants. Yet.

Geopolitical observers call it "mosque diplomacy": a soft-power tool to advance an agenda and foster influence. Among others, Saudi Arabia, Turkey, Qatar, and Iran have sponsored the construction around the world of thousands of mosques as well as *madrassas*—religious schools. The United Arab Emirates has done the same in Indonesia and Kazakhstan, for starters.

I saw this same phenomenon when I was in Tajikistan, the poorest nation in central Asia. I visited an enormous, shiny, $100 million mosque complex in the capital city of Dushanbe. It can hold 120,000 people. I was given a robe and hijab and set free to wander in the then-empty, ornate, human-dwarfing, carpeted mosque that can hold 25,000 worshipers. This vast project was sponsored by Qatar, 1,300 miles away.[f]

Turkey's Directorate of Religious Affairs has, over the past 40 years, systematically financed the construction of more than 100 mosques and schools worldwide, including in Africa. It has also helped to renovate the Mosque of Islamic Solidarity in Somalia—a mammoth mosque that has room for 10,000 worshipers.[g]

Islam is not a monolith. International players advance their own theological agendas. Saudi Arabia, having built mosques in Niger, Nigeria, and Mali, perpetrates Salafism, a stricter interpretation of Islam than that practiced by Sunni Muslims in Turkey, for example.

Meanwhile, Iran has built mosques in Senegal, the Ivory

Coast, and Guinea, among other places. In this competition, Saudi Arabia is building more mosques in Nigeria to counter the Shiite Islam that Iran is attempting to spread. In some areas, this has led to radicalization, which, in one specific mosque, helped the terrorist group Boko Haram to flourish.

But God has His people in place.

Dr. Barnabas Mtokambali is tall, affable, and distinguished. Whether in his conversation or in his preaching, his deep, rolling laughter pours forth when you least expect it. It will make you laugh too. Barnabas's irrepressible wife is named Glad Mary, and her gladness characterizes them both.

Barnabas is president of the Assemblies of God (AG) churches in all of Africa, and archbishop of the AG in his native Tanzania.

Barnabas was born in 1962 in the Njombe region of Tanzania. He grew up in an Anglican, later Roman Catholic family. Young Barnabas was an altar boy and a promising student. He was selected to go to a boarding school, and at age 14 or 15 was studying for a physics exam when a visiting pastor stopped by his dorm room. The pastor pointed at Barnabas's physics book.

"You can read that book and finish it," he said. "But I know a book that you can learn from and never truly finish in a lifetime."

The man pulled a Bible from his bag. Barnabas was curious and a bit shocked; as the pastor talked about how to be born again, he handled his worn Bible with such familiarity, not as if it was an untouchable religious relic.

Barnabas thought he was already saved. Probably. After all, he was an altar boy.

"Thank you for stopping by," Barnabas told the pastor. "I will consider what you have said and make a decision later."

It might have stopped there, but the determined pastor sent another guy. A church elder visited Barnabas, though he waited until after the physics exam.

After three months of questions from Barnabas and answers from the Bible, courtesy of the elder, Barnabas fully opened his heart to Jesus. He soon developed a heavy sense of calling from God to go into church ministry. Barnabas went on to get a BA in Bible and Theology. He was asked to pastor a small church that needed an interim pastor. He fasted and prayed for 21 days about the decision, and during that time, he had a vision.

It was like a dream but unusually clear, and he was awake.

Barnabas saw an area in his town, Morogoro, with a soccer field full of thousands of people. Barnabas was ushered through the huge crowd and taken to a podium in the middle of the field. He heard a voice: "You see all these people. I have given you these people to pastor."

"God's calling is sometimes general but can also be specific," Barnabas says today. He believed God was calling him, for starters, to the small church. It was meeting in a primary school. Five people attended.

Over the years, Barnabas gladly married Glad Mary, started a family, and, even as his church grew, sensed the need for further theological studies. He enrolled in a Master of Divinity program in southern California in 1992. As he finished his MDiv, he faced some challenges back home in Tanzania.

The good news was that that church had grown to about 350 members. The bad news was that though they had acquired a plot of land, they had no permanent building nor the means to build one.

One of Barnabas's seminary friends connected him with some guy named Dois Rosser. Barnabas visited him in

Virginia. He agreed with Dois's biblically orthodox statement of faith and protocols, and they agreed to partner to build Barnabas's church building.

Barnabas went back to Tanzania. In 1997, construction began. Barnabas knew from God that it was to be an "Antioch church." By this, Barnabas—who often speaks in organized outlines, numbering his points on his fingers—meant…

- a church that raised ministers
- a church-planting church
- a prayerful church
- a church of the Word of God
- a church full of the Holy Spirit

In 1998 the Bethel Bible Temple, a 1,500-seat sanctuary, was completed and dedicated to the Lord.

God multiplied and blessed that "Antioch" church. As that local body of believers continued to grow, it began to plant daughter churches. And yes, Barnabas had a list for that:

- Identify places nearby that don't have churches, in order of priority.
- Find a church planter who will stay as pastor.
- Train the leadership, who will serve as the nucleus of the church.
- Commission them.
- Cultivate the community around the plant by whatever means will draw people to hear the gospel, like one-on-one evangelism, evangelistic events, visiting villages and casting out demons. (Note that this last method is not often found in church-planting manuals in the US.)
- Support and care for the church-planting team.
- Reproduce.

As vigorous as the reproductive cycle of Barnabas's church was, his team faced a problem. They needed physical places for their church-plant people to gather in. Meeting under a tree or in a shed or in a structure made of mud and thatch was unsafe, subject to the elements, and did not physically communicate the permanence and power of God in the community.

So Barnabas got back in touch with Dois. He explained his church-planting strategy and the corresponding need for church buildings.

"Yes," said Dois Rosser, always keen to get on board with what God was already starting. "We can help."

"Buildings mean church growth," says Barnabas. "We see this over and over because, when people in a community see a church building, they know the believers are here to stay. Without a building, neighbors don't take you seriously; they just see you as temporary," rather than committed to the long-term good of the community.

Also, Barnabas continues, people want to identify with something magnificent, something of substance. "The nonbeliever views God in light of what the church looks like." Before outsiders encounter Jesus, they see the building, and they draw conclusions about God. "The church building speaks," Barnabas concludes. "The way it is constructed and kept up communicates the gospel."

The church building also brings credibility to the community. In many villages, the churches Barnabas builds are the only attractive, safe, and durable buildings in the hamlet. Government officials ask to use the church building for polling stations. It becomes the center of the community, and the whole village takes pride in it.

Barnabas kept getting promoted in his denomination. Eventually he became president of the Assemblies of God denomination in Africa.

Barnabas says that when he originally partnered with Dois Rosser, there were 1,500 AG churches in Tanzania. At this writing, there are 17,000.

Were all those built in conjunction with ICM? No. But Barnabas says that it's the vision of the partnership—the infectious, energetic building of churches that in turn plant daughter churches that plant daughter churches—that has created this incredible multiplication of investment. The model of cooperative church planting and construction has created a contagious, Holy Spirit mindset of advancement.

Every region of the globe is different in terms of the ethnic, political, and cultural forces at work. And every area is the same in terms of the universality of the gospel as God's great and essential gift for all human beings.

> When people in a community see a church building, they know the believers are here to stay.

Barnabas points out that Tanzania has about 62 million people, with perhaps 35 percent nominal Roman Catholics, 35 percent Muslim, 14 to 20 percent evangelicals and Pentecostals, and roughly one percent animists.

As in other places in the less-developed world, Africans are very open to spiritual things. They know there are unseen realities, and strong forces for both good and evil, beyond the material world we can see and scientifically measure.

So, there is a great appetite for real, biblical Christianity in Tanzania today. But, says Barnabas, there are threats.

The first is that the advance of information technology and the spread of Western values may well lure young people toward a purely secular mindset. As people's economic situation improves, there is also the difficulty of maintaining spiritual fervency and dependence on God as one becomes more materially comfortable.

The second threat, of course, is the militant expansion of

Islam and multiplication of its mosques.

The way to counteract both, says Barnabas, is through strong biblical discipleship. "That's why we are so grateful for Foundations [a comprehensive overview of the Bible]. In my country we use it on radio, as printed literature, for pastoral training, and on audio players for small groups in churches. As people learn the Word of God, miracles are taking place."

Barnabas knows that Christians can't just passively tough times out but should *advance.*

The church is God's distribution system for the gospel.

"The church is God's distribution system for the gospel," he says. "If we don't build churches, we will lose ground to Islam. Tanzania is strategically located to push against its spread. By 2033, our goal is to disciple 7.7 million new believers, to train 35,000 new pastors, and to build 30,000 new churches."

Perhaps that's ambitious. Perhaps it's crazy. But it's congruent with the ancient and only sound strategy to combat the spread of false ideologies like Islam, materialism, and spiritism. Jesus mysteriously said that the gates of hell itself will not prevail against the church He started.[27] That means mere human beings, following His lead, can move forward with His power and peace.

27 Matthew 16:18.

Chapter 9

THE GENEROUS CHURCH AND STRAWBERRIES IN THE DESERT

Remember the words of the Lord Jesus, how he himself said, "It is more blessed to give than to receive."

ACTS 20:35

Tourists from all over the world know Brazil for its beaches and resorts, urban night life, museums, and wildlife habitats. But Brazil's most iconic landmark is the luminous, white, 98-foot-high statue of Jesus set on a mountain overlooking Rio de Janeiro. His arms are 92 feet wide, embracing all who look upon him.

Cristo Redentor—Christ the Redeemer.

But there's a region in Brazil that doesn't draw many tourists nor many Brazilians, who see it as a poor and desolate place. It's called the Sertão, a swath of seven states in the inland northeast. It is subject to frequent droughts, and for those in rural communities, it is difficult to find clean water. Its infrastructure is poor, its people beset by poverty, hunger, drugs, and sexual and physical abuse. Its soil is exhausted, and its people are too. Nominally Roman Catholic, many have no faith perspective apart from occult rituals and a fatalistic sense of desperation. They can't imagine Jesus, bigger than life, His welcoming arms outstretched, toward *them*.

Antônio Torres might be the last person you expect to see in the Sertão. Antônio is a wealthy businessman and a relentless entrepreneur. He has no need to go to a place like the Sertão. But his arms are flung wide to hug every person he encounters there, thumping them on the back, laughing with them as he asks about their family, their story, their concerns. He is a rich guy compelled by Jesus, like Dois Rosser, but has the distinction of being much younger, still alive, and Brazilian. And his story shows how well-to-do churches can help establish and strengthen healthy churches in needy areas.

Antônio grew up poor, in a wooden shack in an inland town. His father was a crop worker and an alcoholic, his mother a spiritist who believed in a vague fusion of reincarnation, good deeds, and African cultism. For good measure, she took her six kids to Mass once a month.

Antônio went to school in the mornings then worked all afternoon and evening. He sold oranges and candy on the street. He polished shoes. He sold popcorn. He was six years old. Many nights his dad would not come home, and Antônio's brothers would go out to find him, passed out in the street, and carry him home.

As the years went by, teenaged Antônio and his brothers sold popsicles, candy, and fruit. His mother did laundry. Seeing new construction in the city, they bought a small cement brick-making machine. They made bricks every night from 7:00 to 11:00 p.m. They saved some money and then started selling sinks, polyglass containers, and water tanks.

Bit by bit, the business grew.

When their company had about 30 employees, Antônio's brother attended a Protestant church. The pastor offered to come to the business every Monday to conduct a devotional service. Antônio didn't know Jesus, but it sounded like a good team-building idea.

Those Monday mornings with the pastor triggered Antônio's energetic curiosity. The pastor invited him to come to church on a Sunday.

"No," said Antônio, "you can come here, but I won't go there because you'll just want me to give money!"

Finally, Antônio visited the church. He opened his heart to Jesus—as did his mother and brothers, one by one.

"It was like a switch flipped inside me," Antônio says today. "Now everything made sense. I gave up drinking, which I was too fond of, like my dad. I saw how everything I have—children, family, business—all belongs to God."

Antônio grew in faith and his understanding of the Bible. He loved his family and church community. His business prospered. He married a wonderful woman, Adriana, who loved Jesus and shared his passion to help others. They gave generously to gospel ministries.

As time went on, his company trucks started to deliver huge water tanks to the Sertão region. His drivers told Antônio of the terrible poverty there. Sometimes they brought home tiny children they had found abandoned on the streets and raised them as their own.

Then the Brazilian government announced an opportunity for private companies to put bids on water cisterns for the Sertão region. Antônio saw it as an opportunity to reach into people's homes and help them.

Before the auction, Antônio met with his pastor and a group of local Christian leaders. They spread out a map of the Sertão like generals plotting a battlefield. They decided that Antônio would bid on the areas with the lowest percentages of Christians.

Antônio's company won a bid for 60,000 cisterns.

"Great!" thought Antônio. "So, I will get to know 60,000 families!"

In 2013 Antônio incorporated two Brazilian nonprofit organizations. One is AMES, a Christian evangelism and church-planting outreach. Because of government strictures, a second organization, *Instituto Água Viva*, focuses on "social work," which flows out of gospel convictions: feeding programs, vocational training, educational enrichment and mentoring, sports outreach, and short-term medical and dental services.

Through Antônio's personal giving, as well as that of other donors, and percentages of his various companies' profits, AMES now sends 380 missionaries into the Sertão. These missionaries are vetted and sent by Brazilian churches outside the Sertão, and benefit from built-in means of accountability, encouragement, and training.

The first time Antônio went to the Sertão himself, he met a man named John Couscous. That wasn't his name, it's just what everyone in his very poor village called him. He was the town drunk.

Couscous's actual name was on the government list of water-assistance program recipients. So Antônio and one of his missionaries, Pastor Danielson, went to his house. It was a dilapidated brown shack, about 12 x 8 feet, with a dark, low ceiling and a crumbling roof.

They knocked, and eventually a girl about twelve years old cracked open the warped door. The story came out that her parents were gone, drunk as usual, and she and her three younger siblings hadn't eaten for several days. The missionary gave them a big basket of rice and beans and other supplies.

As he and Antônio left, promising to return the next day, the girl was starting a fire behind the house to cook the food.

The next day, by the time Pastor Danielson arrived, John Couscous and his wife had stumbled back home. They had been broken with shame when they saw their children eating food generously supplied by strangers. They wanted to change their ways.

The missionary asked if he could hold a service outside their home. "I'll invite the neighbors!" said John... but then he remembered that the whole town thought of him as a belligerent, aggressive drunk. He had no friends.

An engaging guy when sober, John decided to invite people anyway. There was a problem: the closest neighbor was two miles away, and John had let his donkey go a month earlier because he had nothing to feed her.

He started walking. And then, as he looked up the dusty road, there was his missing donkey, ambling toward him as if she was on a mission. He hadn't seen her in 30 days.

"Donkeylita!" shouted John Couscous.

He climbed on and rode to several neighbors' houses.

Only two of the neighbors came to the service that day at the House of Couscous, but John and his family heard the gospel well. They opened their hearts to Jesus.

As time went by, the news got around that John Couscous had changed drastically. The neighbors started coming to little services outside John's house, and eventually they acquired land and built a church. And today at least 500 people have been baptized in John Couscous's dusty but hope-filled church in the Sertão.

Pastor Wellington, who has worked for AMES for ten years in Acauã, the toughest area in the Sertão, says, "Our evangelistic model is based on relationships. Here we have a very religious community. Very syncretistic and superstitious, so there's a lot of resistance to the true gospel. We break through by relationships. We sit with people, drink coffee, and ask about their life stories. We build trust slowly so they start opening up and so we can begin sharing the gospel.

"We try to present Jesus as people's best friend. If we weren't being great friends, going into the dark places where they live, how would people believe that Jesus can be their friend?"

Drugs, prostitution, abuse, and desolation abound in the Sertão. These are tools that Satan uses for his nefarious purposes, as he uses evil all over the world. There is also, as in other developing regions, the overt presence of demonic possession.

Eumar and Júlia Klein are a missionary couple who have been with AMES for years. They regularly visit the ragged homes in the Lapão area, building relationships, praying, and inviting people to join in the community of Jesus followers.

We break through by relationships. We sit with people, drink coffee, and ask about their life stories. We build trust slowly so they start opening up and so we can begin sharing the gospel.

If you travel with them for a day, you may well meet Dinalzida Maria da Conceição Nascimento, whose name is bigger than she is. She is part of the local church. She is tiny, wrinkled, wearing an improbable gray and white ski hat, a delicate pink-flowered blouse over a blue and red dress, and pink flip flops. She has nine grown children including a severely disabled son named Walace, who cannot speak or leave his bed without massive help. She cares for him tenderly, works her crops with her husband, feeds her chickens, and cleans her home, which is decorated with suspended wire cages housing bright equatorial birds. She smiles most of the time and will sing praises to Jesus at the drop of a ski hat.

My next visit was very different. From the street, we could hear berserk, shrieking profanities. There was a narrow passageway, strewn with garbage, and a reinforced concrete structure with thick vertical iron bars in the back of the small house. The screaming intensified the closer we got.

The occupant of the cell was in his mid-twenties, with long, curly black hair, wearing a flimsy pair of gym shorts. His mother, her face hard, her dark brows drawn, said he started using drugs when he was about ten and grew increasingly violent, explosive, and dangerous as he got older. She was wearing a sleeveless top, denim shorts and flip flops, and had defensive wounds on her hands and arms from one of the times he attacked her with a knife. She doesn't know what is wrong with him, but there is nothing anyone can do except keep him away from other people.

Church planters Eumar and Júlia will tell you that the mother doesn't really talk about the whole story. The mom has dabbled in African witchcraft, opening herself up to dark forces, and she refuses to admit the core of her son's problem. She talks about everything else—how her sister wronged her or someone else offended her. The man in the cell screams obscene profanities and filth.

The scene is surreal.

A visiting pastor suggests that the Christians do an exorcism. The AMES people are matter of fact about the situation. After all, Christians in other countries are well familiar with demonic activity, more so than some of us in the West. They tell the visitor that yes, Jesus is supreme over demonic activity, of course. But this home, with the mother and the other siblings, is not protected. They haven't received Jesus and His Holy Spirit.

When you see the dirty cell, hear the shrieking, and consider the mother's resistance to the gospel, Jesus' words become not just a first-century story but a modern reality:

> When the unclean spirit has gone out of a person, it [finds no rest]. Then it says, "I will return to my house" … And when it comes, it finds the house empty, swept, and put in order. Then it goes and brings with it seven other spirits more evil than itself, and they enter and dwell there, and the last state of that person is worse than the first.[28]

The faithful missionaries, Eumar and Júlia, gently pray for the family to open themselves to Jesus. They leave a big container of food. They will be back. They will keep sharing the generous friendship that they have with Jesus.

Perhaps the story that most illustrates the welcome—Jesus' arms spread wide—of the local churches being built in the Sertão is that of a small man named Cicinho.

Cicinho had no home. As a young boy, he was grudgingly taken in by an uncle who brutally abused him. At ten, he was a gang member and a drug mule. Then he became a dealer, and a father at 17. He regularly beat up his woman and broke her fingers. He is a small man, but he carried a big gun. Everyone in his community was afraid of him. For some reason, Cicinho's story is full of drug dealers who counseled him to go straight. The first was the "big dealer," who told Cicinho, "This bravery of yours is taking you to prison or the cemetery. Get out while you can!"

The big dealer was soon killed, and Cicinho did not get out.

28 Matthew 12:43-45.

By the time he'd been in this "life" for 20 years, he was using so much cocaine that he went weeks without sleeping or eating. There was blood in the toilet and stains on his pillow. He put the image of a Catholic saint under his mattress. Maybe she could help him.

One day he even went to a nearby church that AMES had started. He had heard that God heals people. He wanted that, but he was so high that he went back home, got his gun, and returned to yell and wave it at everyone before the pastor arrived. The congregation dispersed for the day.

Later, at home, Cicinho's cousin (with whom he was living and had several children) told him he had a visitor out front.

"He looks like a cop," she said.

Cicinho got his gun and went outside. There was a big, imposing black guy standing a good distance from the house.

"Come closer," called Cicinho, his gun behind his back.

"No," said the guy. "I'm Pastor Eder, from the church you visited."

"Oh!" Cicinho said. He relaxed a bit.

"I want you to know that Jesus loves you," Pastor Eder said.

"Are you sure?" asked Cicinho. "If He loves me, why am I going through this? Why am I chained to this life, bleeding my insides out, unable to sleep or eat or take a deep breath?"

"I'll tell you how He loves you," Pastor Eder responded. "You invite your friends, and we'll have a service right here at your house, and I'll tell everyone."

Cicinho was so stunned he agreed. But he didn't really have any friends. What to do? Ah. He passed the word through the community that he was giving out free cocaine before and after the service to all who came.

The service was packed, but let's just say there was not a vigorous response to the gospel. Afterward, Pastor Eder grinned and hugged Cicinho, whose whole body went stiff with shock.

"I had never been hugged before in my life," he says today. "By anyone. I had feelings I'd never had before."

Cicinho went to church, and people were so friendly. Odd.

At the next church service, Cicinho prayed to receive Christ. That night his desire for drugs was stronger than ever. "God will forgive me," he thought. "But I *have* to do this." Typically, he'd consume 30 to 40 lines of cocaine over time. This night he did one line and passed out on the ground.

It must have been a bad batch, he thought.

Eventually he started vomiting violently, his whole body shaking and convulsing. How could he even be alive? He weighed less than 100 pounds. He told his partner to get rid of all the drugs in all the hiding places of their home.

Not too long after his conversion and deliverance, Cicinho went to a large retreat of AMES pastors, missionaries, and friends in a lovely inn a few hours away by van. He had never traveled this far from where he lived. Antônio Torres had heard Cicinho's story and arranged for him to have the best room in the hotel.

Cicinho stared at the panoramic view out the clean windows of his room, the thick towels, the fresh flowers. He had never experienced anything like this. He had thought of himself, all his life, as less than garbage.

He went back down to the big meeting hall.

"There he is!" someone called, and Cicinho turned to run away. He'd been found out for what he was. Trash.

"No, no, Cicinho, come here," he heard. "Everyone just wants to hear your story. You are so special."

"I had never heard that before in my life," Cicinho says. "I had to carry around a little towel with me all that weekend because I kept crying."

Later Pastor Eder addressed the whole conference at an evening session. "I brought a lot of people here with me this weekend,' he said. 'But one is particularly special. Come up here, Cicinho!'"

Cicinho went slowly to the front, crying into his little white towel. Pastor Eder, bigger than life, his arms stretched wide like Jesus, gathered him up in a huge hug. The whole crowd of the family of God laughed and applauded. Cicinho, like so many in the Sertão, had finally found his way home.

If you're ever fortunate enough to have coffee with Antônio Torres, he can tell you hundreds of stories of what Jesus has started and continues to do, through the churches in the Sertão. As people meet Him, they become part of church communities, grow in discipleship, and reach out to bring others in. It's exponential.

Antônio grins and sketches plans on a big tablet, full of ideas for the next gospel outreach, the next community development. What new crop might they introduce? A year or two ago, Antônio's ministry brought pilot irrigation designs and strawberries to the Sertão, and now 400 poor families have sustaining income from the biggest, reddest, sweetest strawberries you might ever taste. Fruit from the former desert.

"In my long-term vision," Antônio says, "the biggest challenge is to get churches outside the Sertão to understand and engage to meet the obstacles. Unfortunately, many churches in Brazil are focused too much on what's inside their own walls, not outside the walls. Not many put their resources to use for the benefit of those who are outside.

"So, this work is a big challenge. We dream to see 20 percent of the people in the Sertão following Jesus. When we started there, the figure was two percent or less. Now, in some areas, after twelve years of work, it's about ten percent. So, we continue to mobilize churches in comfortable areas to reach into needy areas. We call pastors and invite them to see what God is doing. We pray God would awaken their hearts to send people to the Sertão."

Antônio realizes that the pull of financial comfort and self-involvement is very strong for believers. Two years ago, he began talking with well-to-do Christian entrepreneurs to encourage them to be free to be generous for the Kingdom. "Some of them are starting to think," he says. "But money is a powerful master."

As for Antônio and his house, he has told his four children that he won't be leaving them any inheritance. He has and will help them build their own stories, work hard, enjoy the fruits of their labor, and steward their assets well.

"But for me," he says, "the calling is to give all the resources God has entrusted to me and use them all for His Kingdom. After all, they are His."

Chapter 10

THE ANTIOCH CHURCH

So Barnabas went to Tarsus to look for Saul, and when he found him, he brought him to Antioch. For a whole year they met with the church and taught a great many people. And in Antioch the disciples were first called Christians.

ACTS 11:25-26

So the disciples [in Antioch, hearing of famine in Judea] determined, every one according to his ability, to send relief to the brothers living in Judea. And they did so, sending it to the elders by the hand of Barnabas and Saul.

ACTS 11:29-30

António and the churches in Brazil who are serving the poor in the Sertão are a beautiful example of the generosity—and the joy in giving—that has characterized Jesus' church since its beginnings.

I thought of this—and also of our brother Barnabas in Tanzania, who had consciously modeled his church to be like the Antioch church—when I went to the ancient site of the church in Antioch.

I had not been to Turkey before. It felt huge, mysterious, momentous. Crossroads of both the ancient and modern worlds, it is beautiful, complex, diverse, home to lovely and opinionated people of all sorts.

If you've visited Turkey, you know how poignant it feels to sense the powerful history of Christianity in that place, to travel back in time to an era when the gospel flourished there and then to marvel at the tenacity of the believers who remain even though Christianity has diminished.

Here, in addition to the Antioch church, the early Jesus people founded other churches, like the one in Ephesus, then the third biggest city in the known world. You can still visit the ruins of its great amphitheater, a marble colossus that could seat 24,000 people; you can almost hear the shouts of the incensed Ephesians, railing against Paul when Demetrius, the peeved silversmith, stirred up a riot against him.[29]

After the Roman emperor Constantine legalized Christianity in 313, ending routine Roman persecution of Christians, he moved the capital of the empire from Rome to what would become modern-day Istanbul, which Constantine shyly renamed after himself. (While on a stroll in Istanbul, looking for a thimble of Turkish coffee, I was stunned to see at least one manhole cover labeled "Constantinople," as if it had been put in place millennia earlier. Go figure.)

As the centuries went by and the lines blurred between the official church and the state, history records hard chapters of bloodshed, corruption, and ecclesiastical wealth. The church Jesus started was never meant to fuse with human governments. It shows forth a Kingdom "not of this world," as Jesus said in John 18:36: one based on repentance, belief, and spiritual transformation—not political power.

Turkey officially came under Islamic rule in 1453, and through the years—particularly in the late 19th and early 20th centuries—through a series of horrific pogroms—the

---

29 Acts 19:23-41.

numbers of Christians steadily declined. Between the first quarter of the 20th century to the first quarter of the 21st century, the Christian population of Turkey declined from about 22 percent of the population to 0.2 percent. Today there are an estimated 170,000 to 200,000 followers of Jesus in this country of almost 88 million people.[h]

Leaving Istanbul, I traveled east to Samsun, on the Black Sea; to Gaziantep in south-central Turkey; to Mardin, near the border with Syria; and to Antakya in the west. I met with Jesus followers in all these places. They are part of small local churches that live to show forth the supremacy of Jesus Christ in this Muslim-majority country.

The ancient book-of-Acts city we know as Antioch rests under the modern-day sprawl of Antakya in Turkey's west, north of Syria.

In the first century, Antioch was a sophisticated center of commerce, culture, and government—home to Greeks, Jews, and Romans.

The gospel came there when Jesus followers fled from Jerusalem in the upheaval and persecution that followed the death of Stephen.

> Now those who had been scattered by the persecution that broke out when Stephen was killed traveled as far as Phoenicia, Cyprus and Antioch, spreading the word only among Jews. Some … however … went to Antioch and began to speak to Greeks also, telling them the good news about the Lord Jesus. The Lord's hand was with them, and a great number of people believed and turned to the Lord.[30]

The book of Acts goes on to describe other significant developments that took place in Antioch. The early believers

30 Acts 11:19-21, NIV.

finally saw what Jesus had been saying: the gospel was not only for the Jews. His good news was for all ethnicities and people groups. The promised Kingdom heralded throughout the Old Testament was God's blessing and drawing of the whole world to Himself through the Jews.

No one knows exactly where the ancient church of Antioch met. One possible site is a cave carved into the side of Mount Starius, overlooking modern Antakya. It's a tourist site today.

The early believers finally saw what Jesus had been saying: the gospel was not only for the Jews. His good news was for all ethnicities and people groups.

A church was built in the cave in the fourth or fifth century. Today you can see some pieces of floor mosaics and the faint imprint of frescoes on the walls. There's a tunnel deep inside which opens to a shaft in the mountainside. Perhaps it was used for Christians to evacuate the church if attackers came. Water seeps from a bubbling source beneath the rocks; it was used for drinking and for baptism.

Several Turkish brothers took me there, as well as Anton, my hearty new Russian friend with whom we were traveling, a jovial multilingual pastor who was serving as translator.

I've always felt that stones tell a story; I love how Jesus talked about rocks. On the day of His triumphal entry in Jerusalem, when people were shouting, praising God, blessing Him as King, and the Pharisees told Him to shut them up, He said, "I tell you, if these were silent, the very stones would cry out."[31]

The stones of this ancient church I stood in may or may not have rested on the first-century stones where the apostle Paul—or Peter, the rock-like friend of Jesus Christ who lived for a time in Antioch—preached. But the coolness of the cave, the mossy stones, the soaring roof, and the plain altar erected in the twelfth century—all of it creates a time-travel portal, a connection between us and our ancient legacy.

The day I visited this ancient church with my multinational brothers, other visitors were there too. We were all Christians, as it turned out, from places like Egypt, Germany, Finland, Russia and Romania. Everyone happened to speak English.

Someone suggested that we respond to this ancient place of worship of *Christos*, the Lord Jesus Christ, by singing.

"Yes!" said someone else. "What about 'Amazing Grace'?"

And then it began: a surprising chorus of voices of people who had never seen one another before and would never again in this life, blended in rich harmonies, rising up in the ancient, soaring stones, our song mingling with the hymns once sung in first-century Greek in this very place.

Amazing grace, how sweet the sound,
that saved a wretch like me;
I once was lost, but now am found,
was blind but now I see …
'Twas grace that brought me safe thus far,
and grace will lead me home.

Standing in that echoing cave, I felt the reality we all somehow need to remember, as it will energize us. We really

31 Luke 19:40.

are part of an ancient, international line of Jesus people, stretching unbroken back to the days just after Christ's ascension into Heaven.

Let us not hold our lineage lightly.

Besides its diversity, the ancient Antioch church was also a model of another countercultural characteristic that we saw so clearly in Antonio's work in Brazil: generosity. When famine struck and resources got tight, the church sent financial help to their brothers and sisters in Judea.[32] *If sisters and brothers have needs, we help!*

For those early Christians who had eyes to see, this connected back to one of the key characteristics of the temple in the Old Testament. The temple treasury was to be a means by which the poor, the marginalized, and the defenseless could receive help. God gave His people tithing requirements, gleaning laws, and an overall mandate to support ministry workers and help the poor.[33]

But, in the new covenant, in the upside-down surprise of Jesus Messiah, the temple was not built by human hands. It wasn't a building with a priesthood and a restricted Most Holy Place, where God would come once a year. God had come in Jesus, dwelling among people, His actual presence no longer confined to a religious building but manifest in a community of people, all filled with the actual presence of God through the power of His Holy Spirit, reveling in His constant presence. And it was the community that fulfilled God's heart for the poor, the needy, the defenseless.

The believers understood they were stewards of all that

32 Acts 11:29.

33 See Deuteronomy 14:28-29, for example.

God had entrusted them to manage. They were all about His Kingdom, not the stubby stuff of this world. And if God had poured Himself out for them, how could they not bless others out of the overflow of what they had been given?

It was fitting that I went from Antioch to the center of a horrible natural disaster, one that the modern-day believers in Turkey had responded to with first-century fervor. In them I saw a picture of what the church Jesus started is supposed to do *all the time*: give relief, with love, for those who are outside the church family, that they might be drawn in.

Chapter 11

THE CHURCH THAT IS OUT ON THE STREETS WITH THE PEOPLE

And the master said to the servant, "Go out to the highways and hedges and compel people to come in, that my house may be filled."

LUKE 14:23

The holiest moment of the church service is the moment when God's people—strengthened by preaching and sacrament—go out of the church door into the world to be the church. We don't go to church, we are the church.

ERNEST SOUTHCOTT,
The Church and the World

Later the seismologists would say that it was a 7.8-magnitude earthquake, one of the strongest ever recorded in the region. The confirmed death toll in Turkey alone would be almost 54,000 souls, in the deadliest earthquake there since one in Antioch in AD 526. Scientists would say this was the brutal result of the clashing shift between three tectonic plates under south-central Turkey and northwest Syria, and that the earth shook for 85 seconds.

But for those who experienced it, the horror lasted much longer.

It was the middle of a cold, rainy night, February 6, 2023. Elmas, a dark-haired, middle-aged pastor's wife, was asleep in bed with her husband, Hamdullah. The bedroom pitched and shook, first sideways and then up and down. They huddled together, clutching each other's hands, praying. The noise was what stunned them both. It was like tons of stone crashing together, mountains scraping, a terrible cacophony of raw power unleashed.

And then, finally, it stopped. Temporarily.

Hamdullah grabbed his wallet and car keys. Elmas threw on shoes. All their dishes, pictures, and books had tumbled to the floor, but the walls of their small house were still standing. Elmas thought that perhaps it hadn't been such a bad quake after all. They made their way down the stairs and through their inside courtyard. Then they opened their tall front gate to the street.

Their immediate neighbors lived in six six-story apartment buildings. At that moment, in the rainy haze, Elmas could see that only two of those structures still stood. The other four buildings were nothing but tons of flattened rubble. She could hear faint screaming from those who were buried alive and louder shrieks from neighbors trying to dig people out with their bare hands.

A neighbor who was a strictly observant Muslim, never on the street without her coverings, ran in the rain toward Elmas. She was barefoot, sobbing, wearing only a sleeping shift. "My husband is dead!" she cried. "I cannot find my son!"

Blood was running down her bare arm; one of her fingers was connected by only a scrap of skin. "Please!" she begged Elmas, half out of her mind. "Can you give me a coat and shoes so I can look for him?"

Elmas pulled the anguished woman into her courtyard. She now saw that her own house was crooked and unstable, but all Elmas could think was "Even if I die, I am going to go back up those stairs and get this poor woman a coat so she is covered and does not feel shame."

She picked her way up the stairs, went into her bedroom, and started throwing her blankets, coats, shoes, and clothes down into the open courtyard. Her neighbor got what she needed and rushed back out into the street.

More people were making their way through her front gate, weeping, injured, and cold. Elmas and Hamdullah gave out all their clothes, shoes, and blankets. They held people who couldn't stop shaking. There were sirens, screams, people calling out for their loved ones in the huge piles of concrete, wood, and glass.

There were 570 aftershocks in the first 24 hours, and 30,000 more over the next three months. Elmas and Hamdullah were able to shelter people in their courtyard for 15 days, until the walls of their house finally fell down.

Over those two weeks, Elmas and Hamdullah gave what they could from what they had. Brothers and sisters from churches all over Turkey showed up with bread, water, blankets, and diapers. Humanitarian aid arrived from 94 countries around the world; the Turkish government's disaster relief services rushed to broken villages and cities.

But nothing could ease the pain of realizing, as the terrible days went by, that 350 of their neighbors had died. Elmas had done children's ministry in her neighborhood for years, teaching kids how to write by copying New Testament verses, telling them Bible stories, and feeding them snacks and tea. Now she watched in horror as rescue workers pulled small bodies from the rubble. They were children Elmas had hugged and fed, kids she had last seen laughing and playing. And now they were twisted and still. The workers didn't have enough body bags for them all.

In the grueling weeks and months that followed, Elmas and Hamdullah and their fellow believers barely slept, pouring themselves out to help survivors however they could.

Miraculously, their new five-story church building under construction was still standing, though buildings all around it had toppled.

"People were open to hearing about Jesus because we were with them in their bad days. They came to pour out their troubles and cry with us, also to share a meal, have some tea, even laugh together. Maybe they just wanted help, but their hearts were open."

As the long months went by, the Turkish believers, though fatigued, were constant. "I'm amazed we are still standing," says Elmas.

She continues, "Last week 1,000 people came to the church. We're having women's meetings, kids programs, men's gatherings, and teen ministries. The other day at church, we asked, 'Who wants to receive Jesus?' and 20 people came to the front.

"I'm hearing the footsteps of revival. We don't know how long we'll have this period—this open window. So, whatever, however, wherever we can, we should show forth Jesus because we have limited time."

Zilan is one of those people reached during this "open window." She decided to follow Jesus because of the love of the Christians.

She's a slender, young woman who talks with her hands and laughs a lot. For Zilan, the earthquake itself was not as traumatic as Elmas' experience. She was a teenager; she slept through it. Her Muslim family, including her oldest brother and his wife, lived together in one house. Her other brother was in college, and her father was working in Sudan to provide for the family. All Zilan remembers is that on the night of the quake, her brother's wife, who was eight months pregnant, rushed into her bedroom, shouting.

"Let me sleep," mumbled Zilan.

But then other people were running in and out, her sister-in-law wouldn't stop screaming, and Zilan sat up, now worried that her sister-in-law would go into premature labor.

They ran out into the street. And then their house fell down.

Zilan and her family lived in their car for 20 days. Then they got a tent in a camp of temporary dwellings. Though life was upside down, Zilan still had her phone, and she saw on Instagram that Christians were distributing wooden houses the size of a small trailer. That would be a step up. She didn't know anything about Christians, but she got in touch with the guy on the post, a pastor named Paul.

> We don't know how long we'll have this period—this open window. So, whatever, however, wherever we can, we should show forth Jesus because we have limited time.

Pastor Paul is middle-aged, a competent and reassuring presence, and when the ground first rumbled and shook, he swung into action. Before he was a pastor, he had been a soldier, and during Turkey's big earthquake back in 1999, he had been deployed to help survivors. So, he knew what would be needed and the types of trauma that people would experience.

In the beginning, as people were settling into temporary tent camps, Paul did the most basic things. He distributed bread, simply going from tent to tent handing out loaves to family groups. Despite the urge to hurry, he took his time, greeting people, learning their names, praying for those who were open to it.

> Even in trauma, life is always all about relationships, and people are touched by the attitude of love more, in fact, than just the need for bread.

One day the leader of a 45-member family group of quake refugees from Syria came to Paul and hugged him hard.

"I wish I could do more," said Paul. "It's only bread."

"You don't understand," the man told him. "I was out yesterday where an NGO was distributing help, and when my turn came in the line, I didn't even take anything, I was so angry and upset. The workers were shouting at us to hurry up, cursing, treating us like animals, like we weren't even human beings. So, I just came back to the tent.

"But you are different," the man told Paul. "You talk with us. You treat us with respect. What organization are you from?"

Paul explained that he wasn't part of an organization, that he and his friends were just followers of Jesus from a local church. The man had never heard of such a thing but hugged him again.

"I had thought they needed physical things more than spiritual things," Paul said later. "But I realized, even in trauma, life is always all about relationships, that people are touched by the attitude of love more, in fact, than just the need for bread."

Certainly, that attitude of love is what touched the bubbly teenager Zilan. When she connected with Pastor Paul about tiny wooden houses, he introduced her to a pastor and his wife who had come from Istanbul to help people in the tent and container camps. The couple told Zilan about Jesus. Zilan had never heard of Him. She called Paul and asked if he could give her a New Testament. He did.

"Once I started reading, I couldn't stop," Zilan says today. "I had this notebook I could write my thoughts in, and whenever I found a verse I liked, I would copy it down."

The pastor's wife from Istanbul invited Zilan to come to a youth conference in Istanbul to hear more about the gospel.

So improbably, Zilan and her college-age brother, who was in Antakya for the summer months, went to the Christian youth conference in Turkey's main city. Their parents didn't know much about it but were glad for the kids to have a break from the rubble and chaos of Antakya.

At the retreat site, the pastor's wife saw Zilan's journal with its Scripture quotes and asked her if she'd like to become a believer in Jesus.

Zilan asked her to wait a minute, left the room, and called her friend Pastor Paul. "What is it to become a Christian?" she asked Paul. "Should I do that?"

Paul laughed on the phone. "It's a good thing," he said.

Zilan went back to the older woman. "Okay," she told her. "I'm ready!"

Zilan's brother snorted at her when she prayed to received Jesus, but then, late that night, he had a dream. A powerful dream. He never told Zilan what it was but shared his vision with the pastor the next day. Then he repented of his sins and prayed to follow Jesus.

On the way home from the conference, Zilan and her brother suddenly realized something important.

In her words, "We forgot about our family! Now what? We're Muslim!"

"Okay," said her brother. "We hide this. We just won't tell them."

The only problem was that Zilan is very bad at keeping secrets.

They arrived back to their container camp.

"What did you do at the conference?" asked their mother.

"Oh, not much," said Zilan's brother. "We walked around Istanbul."

Their mother turned toward Zilan. "Anything else?"

"Uh, well, we became believers in Jesus!" Zilan blurted out.

The ensuing conversation did not go well.

Zilan's brother soon went back to college in Crete, so Zilan was the focus of her parents' concern. Since they were nominal rather than fervent Muslims, they were less angry about her choice and more worried that she'd joined some sort of Western cult.

Eventually Zilan's mother started attending Pastor Paul's church, in order to investigate just what it was her daughter had gotten into. To Zilan's surprise, the investigation was thorough. Her mom came back week after week. And what Zilan did not know was that her dad, now back in Antakya with them, had started listening to the audio New Testament in Turkish on his phone. He started coming to church to "investigate" as well.

The church held weekly Bible studies on Tuesdays. One night after the Bible lesson, as usual, Zilan went into the small kitchen to prepare snacks for everyone. She came out to the main meeting room with a tray in her hands… and then, surprise, there were both of her parents, standing in front of the church, laughing toward her with tears in their eyes.

Zilan stood still with her tray, staring at them.

"We have decided to follow Jesus too," her father announced.

If you ask Zilan about how Jesus has changed her life, she has a flood of answers. But the first thing she told me was this: "Before, I was jealous of everyone. But Jesus helped me—now I don't compare myself with others, and I feel free."

If you know any teenaged girls, you know that this is a miracle.

There are so many stories I could tell, but let me conclude with the words of Pastor Selim, whom I interviewed after sharing lunch with Zilan,

Pastor Selim is a distinguished man with a white goatee, a leader among the band of pastor-brothers like Pastor Paul in this part of Turkey. His many years of ministry in hard soil have not always overflowed with converts, but the terrible earthquake in Turkey taught the churches something important, he says.

Right after the disaster, Pastor Selim told his small congregation that of course they would figure out how to give people in need whatever they lacked. But he continued, "What is important is that we give bread, water, shoes, whatever… with *the love and the humility of Jesus*. If we just give the things, we're no different from the government giving the things."

And that ministry to those outside the church created a new sense of mission and identity for those inside the church.

"The earthquake destroyed many things," says Pastor Selim. "Buildings. Walls. It also destroyed the walls between people. Before, we had walls between Orthodox and Catholic and Protestant and Muslims. We had all been living behind our walls, but the earthquake tore them down.

"So, it is good. Because of this earthquake, the church got out from behind its four walls. We were out on the street, with the people."

Chapter 12

THE CHURCH THAT SOWS SEEDS IN HARD SOIL

For still the vision awaits its appointed time; it hastens to the end—it will not lie. If it seems slow, wait for it; it will surely come; it will not delay.

HABAKKUK 2:3

In the aftermath of Turkey's terrible earthquake, local Christians poured themselves out, meeting the ministry opportunities that tragedy makes possible.

In other parts of Turkey, believers pour themselves out daily in less dramatic ways, patiently trying to cultivate faith in the hard soil. We can learn much from their perseverance, tenacity, and creativity as they operate within the restrictions of their culture. They are playing the long game, doing everything they can, waiting on the Lord.

I saw this when I spent time with a man who, ironically, used to play the short game. He was ready to give his life in a flash, whenever he was called into action. Political action.

He's the first pastor I've met who trained to be a suicide bomber.

Azad[34] is a bearded, middle-aged man with thoughtful eyes,

34 Azad is a pseudonym.

white teeth, and a big smile. I met him in the ancient, lofty walled city of Mardin, which looks out over Syria. You can almost see the footsteps of Abraham and other Old Testament patriarchs shimmering on the dusty plains below.

Azad is from the eastern part of Turkey. He's a Kurd and grew up speaking the Zaza language in his Sunni Muslim family. His dad and older brother were part of the PKK, a radical Marxist-Leninist Kurdish resistance group, committed at the time to securing a Kurdish independent state. They had both spent time in jail for their cause.

Azad spent a lot of time with his uncle, going to Muslim prayers and reciting the Qur'an in Arabic. As a teenager, he got hold of a Turkish version of the Qur'an.

"Uncle," he said to his father's brother, "why are we Muslims?"

His uncle took another sip of tea. "Because we were born in a Muslim place."

Azad pressed on. "Well, how do we know Islam is right?"

His uncle shrugged. "We're Muslims because our fathers were Muslims."

"Okay," said young Azad, "let's say there is a 90 percent possibility we are right. What happens if it turns out we're in the ten percent and we're wrong?"

"Well, we'll go to hell," said his uncle.

"What?" Azad sputtered. "Does that mean we are leaving to chance this possibility we could go to hell? We aren't even investigating these other religions!"

"What do you propose?" his uncle asked.

"Let's pray," said Azad. "Let's pray that God will show us the right way!"

From then on, after his formal prayers in the mosque, Azad would plead with God: "I just want to come to You. Show me the right way!"

He heard nothing. Meanwhile, he'd started to read the

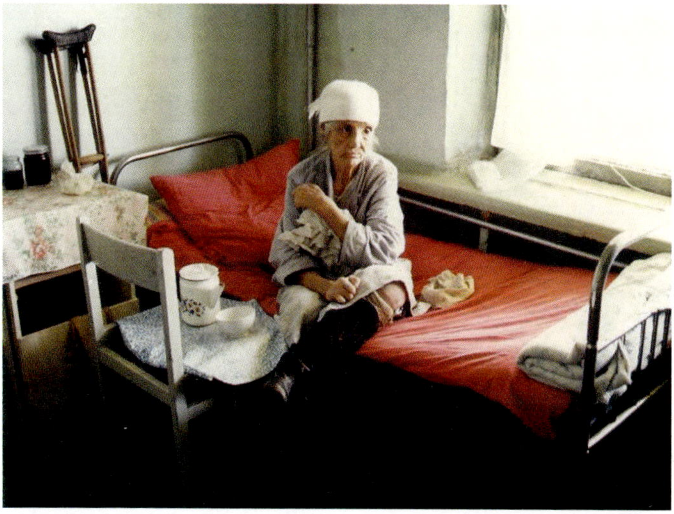

Gulshamal *(Chapter 1)*

Omer *(Chapter 2)*

Tatiana *(Chapter 5)*

Hospitality from a pastor's family in Tajikistan *(Chapter 5)*

Gobohor, a lay leader in Tatiana's church *(Chapter 5)*

Yashar *(Chapter 7)*

Dois Rosser *(Chapter 6)*

Dois Rosser with children in Cambodia *(Chapter 6)*

Dr. Barnabas Mtokambali *(Chapter 8)*

Dois Rosser with Barnabas, U.S. supporters, and enthusiastic parishioners at the dedication of a new church in Tanzania in the early 2000s *(Chapter 8)*

Antônio Torres in a vineyard he planted in the Sertão *(Chapter 9)*

Life in the Sertão (Chapter 9)

Dinalzida Maria da Conceição Nascimento (Chapter 9)

Cicinho *(Chapter 9)*

Brazilian missionary and church planter Júlia Klein reaching out to the lost with the love and power of Christ *(Chapter 9)*

The Cave Church of Saint Peter, traditionally considered the spot where the apostle Paul first preached the gospel in ancient Antioch, and a great place to sing "Amazing Grace" *(Chapter 10)*

Elmas *(Chapter 11)*

The church that stood in the earthquake *(Chapter 11)*

Zilan *(Chapter 11)*

Pastor Paul *(Chapter 11)*

Pastor Selim *(Chapter 11)*

Pastor Azad *(Chapter 12)*

Pastor Ahmet Guvener,
in Azad's church *(Chapter 12)*

Matias, Ellen, Pastor Stephen *(Chapter 13)*

A fisherman mends his nets outside his home,
Nkombo Island *(Chapter 14)*

Nkombo church kids' feeding program *(Chapter 14)*

Nkombo women in joyful worship *(Chapter 14)*

Worship in a women's vocational training and sewing class,
Rwanda *(Chapter 14)*

Cellphone photo from a pastor showing bomb damage to the apartment home of some of his parishioners *(Chapter 15)*

Daria and Denys *(Chapter 15)*

Baptism day for Yevgenij and Tatyana, along with other converts and their pastors *(Chapter 15)*

Isaac Acire *(Chapter 16)*

Eunice *(Chapter 16)*

Women's empowerment program *(Chapter 16)*

Paska and her son *(Chapter 16)*

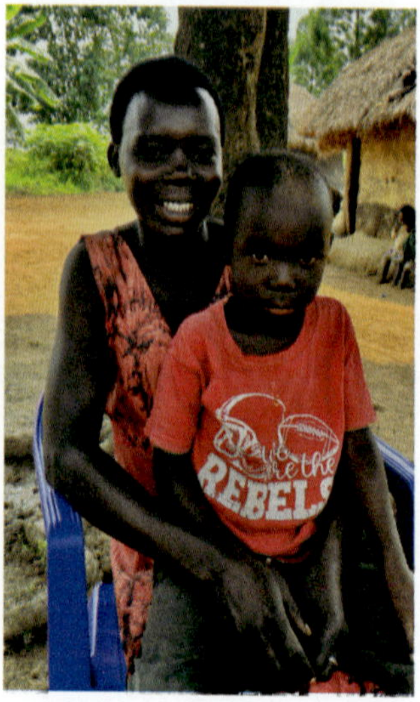

Gloria and Ellen *(Chapter 16)*

A church that was burned by extremists *(Chapter 17)*

A pastor's young daughter's doll in the charred ruins of the family's home *(Chapter 17)*

Qur'an in his own language, rather than just reciting portions of it in Arabic, which he didn't understand. Now, as he discovered the message, he didn't like what he was reading. He thought, "If this is the god of Islam, then I don't believe in God." He became an atheist.

But he was still a zealot for his people. He got more involved with the PKK. At first, he gathered food supplies and clothes for the guerrillas who were hiding in the mountains. At 18, he started writing for a Kurdish newspaper. Then he joined the PKK military wing. He was sent to Urmia, in northern Iran, for military and ideological training. There he read communist literature, Darwin, and parts of the New Testament—which was available so fighters could acquaint themselves with the holy book of the infidels.

He was sent to northern Iraq in 2000 and got further training in all kinds of weapons, including explosives. Out of 16,000 PKK fighters at the time, 70 were chosen to be on the most elite fighting team of all: the suicide bombers.

As an atheist, Azad had no religious motivation, no fervor for *jihad* or a ticket straight to Muslim paradise. He was simply willing to die for what he saw as the Kurdish cause, for the love of his people. He was provided no psychological training for his mission, nor would he know what it was until the time came. Perhaps an attack on a military installation. When he would eventually trigger his explosive vest and the end would come, Azad thought he would feel the ripping force of metal and flame… and then nothing. Nothing. He was okay with that.

But before Azad could carry out his assignment, he was arrested in northern Iraq for his connection with the PKK. He was sent to Turkey for a twelve-year prison term. He was 21. In prison he read the New Testament, still wondering if there just might be something to it. He decided that if he ever got out of prison, he'd go to a Christian church.

At the time, Azad says, Turkey was trying to get into the European Union, and the EU did not look well on jailing people simply for their associations, people who had not yet committed any crime. So, Azad was released from prison. He returned to his home in Lice, in the eastern part of Turkey.

One Sunday he walked all over his town, looking for a church. It wasn't as if there were signs on the street: "Church this way." He could not find one. Ditto the next Sunday.

Finally, on the third Sunday, he saw a cross and a bell in a tower; it was an Assyrian Orthodox church. Azad had a notepad with him. On it he'd jotted his 20 most pressing questions about God.

Services were over, but Azad knocked on the church door. A priest opened it.

"I have some questions I want you to answer," said Azad.

"Are you a student?" asked the priest.

"You could say that."

"Come in," said the priest.

They sat down on a hard pew.

"In Islam," Azad began, "the premise is that God made people to test them. Do you believe that?"

"Yes," said the priest.

Azad went on. "In Islam, God has written your life, and that's it. Do you believe in fate?"

"Yes," said the priest.

"Does God know everything?"

"Yes," said the priest.

Azad frowned. "But if God knows everything and He wrote my fate, then why is He testing us? What's the point of the test if it's all pre-determined?"

"What?" said the priest. "I've got other things to do."

"Do you have a New Testament?" asked Azad.

"No!" said the priest.

Azad left. This was no good. So disappointing.

But a small voice inside of him was saying, "That priest didn't know anything. There must be people who know. Go find them."

The next Sunday, Azad went back to the same area and looked across the alley. He saw what he didn't see before: a Protestant church. Might as well check it out.

He knocked and was welcomed inside by a Turkish pastor named Ahmet and Jerry, a visiting American who loves the Turkish people.

Azad got out his notebook. For each question, the two men showed him answers from the Turkish Bible. He stayed for almost three hours. They had tea. He asked if they had a New Testament; they gave him a whole Bible.

"I will read it," Azad told them. "And I'll have questions. Can I come again? But I need you to know who I am. If you tell me that my past is too bad and you don't want me to come back, I'll understand."

He told them his story.

"Okay," said Ahmet. "Everybody has sinned. God forgives us. Our door is always open. Come!"

Ahmet Guvener has been a well-respected Christian leader in Turkey for decades, faithfully pastoring, mentoring, and preaching the gospel on the radio and satellite TV. He's survived two assassination attempts.

A spiritual father and grandfather to many in the 24 churches in this part of Turkey, Ahmet is to Azad what the apostle Paul calls God's "living letter." (Paul wrote to the members of the church of Corinth in 2 Corinthians 3:2-3, "You yourselves are our letter of recommendation, written on our hearts, to be known and read by all … written not with ink but with the Spirit of the living God, not on tablets of stone but on tablets of human hearts.")

Azad served for several years as a deacon in Ahmet's church. Then, in 2013 he was sent out to start a church in Mardin, near the Syrian border. He developed and led a fellowship that met in a house, and today Azad is the pastor of one of the oldest Protestant churches in the Middle East.

Founded in 1860 by American missionaries, the church originally served Assyrian Christians worshiping in Syriac or Aramaic—the language related to that spoken by Jesus. But eventually the building fell into disrepair and sat empty for 70 years. By God's grace and hard work on Azad's part, permission was granted to the Protestant community to use it.

Restored and reopened in 2016, the Mardin Protestant church hosts Sunday services, women's gatherings on Tuesdays, and is open all week for tourists—providing a unique opportunity to cast gospel seed to Muslim visitors from all over Turkey.

Mardin is a UNESCO World Heritage Site. There are famous mosques and *madrassas* (places of study) throughout the city, and Mardin is a destination for many Turkish sightseeing tours.

The tourists troop through Mardin's charming cobblestone streets, sip Turkish coffees, and visit historic places, including Pastor Azad's Protestant church. Few of the visitors have ever set foot in a church.

Pastor Azad is there to welcome them. He points out highlights of the beautiful building and answers questions. You can see him with clumps of six to twelve Turkish tourists at a time. The people are curious about Christianity, what Christians believe, and how it differs from Islam, and this historic Christian site is a safe place to ask questions.

Pastor Azad answers those questions and gives every visitor who wants one a paperback copy of the *Incil*—the New Testament in Turkish. You see them in people's hands or sticking out of their backpacks as they leave. Some even stay for a cup of coffee and further conversation.

"We give out between eight and ten thousand New

Testaments a year," says Azad. "We have no way of knowing what happens through them. And sometimes I feel discouraged. I know that I can do all things through Christ who gives me strength, but the soil is so hard here in Turkey. We don't know what God is doing at any point in time. But we trust in Him."

So, Pastor Azad continues to faithfully sow the seed of the gospel wherever he can, however he can, in the fertile soil of his church members as well as among those whose hearts may or may not be ready for harvest.

When you leave his stone church, you'll see bright flowers blossoming in pots along the narrow walled passageways. A saddled donkey is standing near the doorway, just in case you need one.

> Pastor Azad continues to faithfully sow the seed of the gospel wherever he can, however he can, in the fertile soil of his church members as well as among those whose hearts may or may not be ready for harvest.

And just down the passageway and around the corner, you'll see an unusual signpost. It's a vertical pole with painted wooden arrows mounted horizontally.

"Latifiye Camii," reads the first arrow. Latifye Mosque, built in 1371, that way.

"Ulu Camii," reads the second. Grand Mosque, built in the 12th century, to the left.

Seyh Cabuk Camii. Sheik Jabuk Mosque, built in the 1500s, that way.

And the remaining arrow?

"Kilisesi." Church. Yes, if you want to come into the Christian church, step right this way.

This may well be one of the few places in the Islamic world where people are pointed not only to the mosques but also to the church that Jesus started.

Chapter 13

THE CHURCH AS THE HOUSE OF RECONCILIATION

I knew that to really minister to Rwanda's needs meant working toward reconciliation in the prisons, in the churches, and in the cities and villages throughout the country. It meant feeding the hungry, sheltering the homeless, caring for the young, but it also meant healing the wounded and forgiving the unforgivable. I knew I had to be committed to preaching a transforming message to the people of Rwanda. Jesus did not die for people to be religious. He died so that we might believe in Him and be transformed … I was called to that—proclaiming the message of transformation through Jesus Christ.

JOHN RUCYAHANA, *The Bishop of Rwanda: Finding Forgiveness Amidst a Pile of Bones*

In contrast to the hard spiritual soil of Turkey, consider the rolling, green hills of Rwanda, the tiny east-central African nation.

Perhaps you've visited Rwanda. It's a jewel of a country. Many of us have enjoyed its cleanliness, great coffee, community pride, and the marvelous hospitality of the many believers there. In one sense, its notorious genocide—nearly a million Rwandans killed by fellow Rwandans in three months—seems too ugly and remote to think about. Why focus on something that happened back in 1994?

But the government, church leaders, and people of Rwanda think it is important to remember.

First, if a nation forgets or denies its past evils, it is more likely to repeat them. And second, for actual healing from trauma to take place, both individually and nationally, the wrongs of the past must be seen, their devastation acknowledged, and purposeful steps taken toward restorative justice, recovery, and reconciliation.

In this, the people of Rwanda have much to teach the rest of us.

The beginnings of the 1994 genocide are still murky. There were two main tribal designations in Rwanda: the Tutsi minority and the Hutu majority. Anti-Tutsi violence had broken out in prior years. Evidently, dark plans for ethnic cleansing had long been laid. Outside weapons had slipped into the country. Crude pamphlets circulated, oozing with propaganda that dehumanized and denigrated Tutsis. And on the night of April 6, 1994, the airplane carrying the Hutu president of Rwanda, Juvénal Habyarimana, was shot down just before it landed in Kigali. Assassination by unknown elements. Blame fell on the Tutsis. The next morning Hutu killing squads disposed of the Tutsi prime minister and her husband, as well as moderate Hutu leaders.

Hate speech against Tutsis—called "cockroaches"—poured from a popular radio station: "Rwanda is a Hutu land. We are the majority. They are a minority of traitors and invaders. We will squash their infestation."[i] Hundreds of thousands of machetes had been imported from China and distributed to militia members all over the country. District organizers presided over the low-tech killings. The goal was to leave no Tutsi—and no Hutu who protected or sympathized with Tutsis—alive in Rwanda.

Armed gangs of young paramilitaries called the *Interahamwe* set up roadblocks; people had to show their IDs to pass. If their tribal designation—or their appearance—did not please the killers, they were slaughtered on the street. Men, women, and children fled to churches for sanctuary. They were bludgeoned, burned, and beheaded between the pews and in front of the altars. A half-million women were raped.

Now, three plus decades later, the people of Rwanda are determined to help one another heal from their horrible past and to move forward together.

That is possible only if those Rwandans choose the route of confession and forgiveness rather than denial and retribution—a path that local churches are uniquely equipped to share, through the power of the Holy Spirit.

Here's one story,[j] among so many, of what that can look like.

Two ordinary Rwandans named Gahigi Stephen and Sendageya Matias were neighbors in a small village near Rwanda's border with Burundi. Stephen, a Tutsi, was tall and slender with a broad smile. A pastor, he had a wife and children and a small farm. He raised cows.

Matias, a Hutu, was shorter than Stephen, with widely spaced dark eyes, a humble manner, and an occasional shy smile. Once, when he saw that Matias was in need, Stephen gave him a cow, which, in Rwanda, can make a big economic difference in a person's life because of milk, manure, and other benefits.

In April 1994 Pastor Stephen knew that something terrible was going to happen. He had heard about killings in other areas. And in the countryside, the machetes had all been sharpened.

One night Stephen and his family fled from their home. If they could only get to the border with Burundi, perhaps they'd be safe. They and other Tutsis from the village ran through fields of sorghum and pushed desperately through thick jungle bushes in the darkness.

They neared the border. There was a burst of gunfire. Stephen saw friends and neighbors running one second and then punched down by bullets the next, lying still in the dirt. Stephen and his family were surrounded. Stephen saw his Hutu neighbor Matias in the darkness, a machete in his hand. His face did not look right.

"I was filled with hate," Matias says today. "The government supported us; they told us to go and kill. The district officials told us to get going, do your work, kill the Tutsis, massacre them all."

Matias was 37 at the time. He felt like Satan was twisting his mind.

> Stephen realized that forgiveness was not just a nice choice that good Christians should do. No, it was *life* for him.

"I was in a terrible state. I would kill people and take their clothes.

"I went to Pastor Stephen's family with so much hate. I wanted to do harm even though he had given me a cow. I killed the rest of his cows. I killed six of his family."

In the dark chaos of that horrific night, Stephen was separated from his family. He ran again through the bush. He heard a child crying. He stopped. In the dim light he could see a little boy, about four years old, whimpering near the base of a tree, blood all over him.

"My heart!" Stephen says with tears, all these decades later. In his confusion and terror, he had not even recognized his own son. He rushed to the tree and knelt in the dirt. He whispered to the child, "Who am I? Who am I?"

"Papa!" cried his son.

Stephen scooped him up and ran and ran and ran. He and his son made it to Burundi.

When the genocide was over and more than 800,000 people lay dead, Stephen returned to his village. Along with tens of thousands of his fellow perpetrators, Matias was arrested and thrown into prison.

Stephen had survived, but each day was excruciating. "How could innocent people be killed like this?" he says. "I was full of hate. I didn't want to see or hear people like Matias. So much pain. In Rwandan culture, men are not supposed to cry. I had my life and my little son and my wife; I was lucky. But I had lost my aunties, my parents, my sisters. I was hungry. I was poor. Nothing!"

It was hard to pray. But Stephen did, pouring out his pain to God. Silence. Then, one night Stephen felt God say to him, "I want to take away your pain. I have preserved you to use you. I want to use you to show My glory."

Stephen wept and punched his fists in the dirt. He sobbed all night. Then, impossibly, in the morning, "I began to feel a new mind," he says. "Christ, on the cross, said, 'Father, forgive them; they don't know what they're doing.' My boss Jesus Christ went through this. I began to take small steps."

Stephen realized that forgiveness was not just a nice choice that good Christians should make. No, it was *life* for him. Without it, he would spend the rest of his allotted years in a slow, bitter monotony of mental torture, his heart a stone within him.

Stephen knew that forgiving Matias was not dependent on any action on Matias's part. This was a transaction, an act of obedience, between Stephen and God. Stephen also knew that in his own strength or willpower, he could not forgive. But he could be *willing*. And Christ would have to share His power with Stephen.

It wasn't merely an internal spiritual process. It required small steps, actually *doing* what Stephen perceived God was telling him to do.

So, Pastor Stephen went to preach the gospel at the stinking, overcrowded prison where Matias and other killers were behind bars. Matias saw Stephen in the crowd in the prison yard. He hid. He knew Stephen had come to kill him.

On his next prison visit, Stephen did find Matias. He told him a few simple facts. Because of Jesus, Stephen told Matias, he had forgiven him for killing his family.

Further, he told Matias that if he repented, *God* would forgive him. God could make him new, heal his heart, take away the stain of his guilt.

No. Matias couldn't believe it. Too good to be true. Impossible.

But, as Stephen kept coming back, Matias began to believe. He confessed his crimes to God, Stephen, and government authorities. He told Stephen where he had thrown his family members' bodies on that dark night years earlier. Stephen felt a measure of closure that he could bury their remains.

Matias was released from prison after serving almost ten years. Now he is in his late sixties. He sees the darkness of his past as the prequel to God's healing and the miracle of his relationship with Stephen in simple, concrete terms: "Now Stephen and I are friends. He drives me in his car; I share food with him. We celebrate holidays together."

When he and Stephen go to church together, Matias says, "The church speaks truth that brings us freedom. If you can't let go of the guilt, you will never be healed. The church has helped us to see that. God saw my heart in the beginning, and now He has seen my repentance… my heart is free now, and we want to carry this message of forgiveness and reconciliation all over Rwanda."

I first met Stephen and Matias a few years ago, in Kigali. I visited with them again just a few months ago. And each time I'm with them, their story somehow seems more real, their brotherhood deeper. Matias, in particular, had more joy and peace on his face than when last I saw him. Again, he isn't a philosophical guy; he speaks in ordinary terms about how his past has been utterly canceled out by Christ.

At this point in his life, he told me, "I can't even use a machete to cut grass or a tree. If someone said, 'Here, use this *panga* to slaughter a cow for meat in the village,' I would say, 'No, kill me first. I cannot do it.'"

And Pastor Stephen, who knows deeply that forgiveness and a desire for reconciliation don't come from human determination but from the power of the Holy Spirit, says this: "After the genocide I had many enemies. Now, because I forgave, I have no enemies. And I have a friend. Matias."

The Right Reverend Nathan Amooti Rusengo, the Anglican bishop of Kigali, is all about the same reality: because Jesus is our Friend, we can be friends with one another in the most unlikely and elemental way.

Nathan is a tall, jovial man with a hearty laugh. With his large, gold cross, flowing robes, and shepherd's crook, he has overseen overflowing churches for decades.

"All our people have scars," he says. Some of those scars are visible, like the puckered gashes where a machete sliced a young boy's cheek or the bullet wounds many soldiers still bear. But the more significant scars are internal, as those borne by the women who were raped, the children who lost their parents and are now parents themselves, the villagers whose homes were burned and whose loved ones were killed. Bishop Nathan's own brother died in the genocide.

But Bishop Nathan, like his friends Stephen and Matias, sees that forgiveness is not just a nice option for those who want to be extra-obedient to God. It is the practical necessity for life and healing. And the local church can be the house for reconciliation.

> Through the Holy Spirit, our churches can be fruitful greenhouses of reconciliation and love in splintered communities, rather than falling into the world's perpetual trap of retribution, tribalism, and divisive hatred.

"We cannot bring back those who died," he says, "But for those of us who are still alive, let us live in peace. The love of God, through the church, has brought enemies together and heals their children and their children's children. This is the future of our church and the future of our country."

When Bishop Nathan and his fellow church leaders heard some years ago that the Rwandan government was at the time actively promoting "reconciliation," they stepped up to help people like Stephen and Matias. They knew the church can accomplish certain things that no government can.

"We as church people got excited because ours is a ministry of reconciliation, according to 2 Corinthians," says Nathan. "Everywhere we spoke—in pulpits, prisons, schools, everywhere—we preached that we are human beings, created in the image of God, with the agency to forgive because of what He has done."

Because God has reconciled us to Himself, we can have peace with Him. We can have the power of His Holy Spirit.

We can forgive others because God forgave us. Like Gahigi Stephen.

Wherever we live and whatever we've suffered, we, too, can participate in this "ministry of reconciliation." When the Holy Spirit led the apostle Paul to exhort believers to do so, his words were not only for the first-century church but for those of us who follow Jesus 2,000 years later.

This is hard—just as it is in modern Rwanda or was in first-century Corinth. But, as Paul wrote to the Corinthian church, "Therefore, if anyone is in Christ, he is a new creation. The old has passed away; behold, the new has come."[35]

As Christ's new creations, we bear the fruit of the Holy Spirit: love, joy, peace, patience, kindness, goodness, faithfulness, gentleness, and self-control.[36]

> All this is from God, who through Christ reconciled us to himself and gave us the ministry of reconciliation; that is, in Christ God was reconciling the world to himself, not counting their trespasses against them, and entrusting to us the message of reconciliation. Therefore, we are ambassadors for Christ, God making his appeal through us.[37]

Through the Holy Spirit, our churches can be fruitful greenhouses of reconciliation and love in splintered communities, rather than falling into the world's perpetual trap of retribution, tribalism, and divisive hatred. In this polarized and politically angry season in the West, it's a great time for believers to be freshly reminded that God has entrusted *His* ministry of reconciliation *to us*. It is the church's role to preach Jesus' radical gospel of forgiveness and to practice it lavishly.

---

35 2 Corinthians 5:17.

36 Galatians 5:22-23.

37 2 Corinthians 5:18-20.

Chapter 14

THE CHURCH THAT COMFORTS THE AFFLICTED

Blessed be the God and Father of our Lord Jesus Christ, the Father of mercies and God of all comfort, who comforts us in all our affliction, so that we may be able to comfort those who are in any affliction, with the comfort with which we ourselves are comforted by God.

For as we share abundantly in Christ's sufferings, so through Christ we share abundantly in comfort too.

2 CORINTHIANS 1:3-5

My friend Bertha embodies this lavish biblical ministry of reconciliation. Bertha is a strong, sturdy, smiling Rwandan woman with beautiful braids and a steady gaze, an Anglican priest. She, like so many, lost numerous family members in the genocide. And she, like so many, has experienced further betrayal and trauma that fuels her ministry to traumatized women.

Bertha grew up in a dysfunctional home. Her dad was abusive. As a teenager, she went to live in the home of a trusted member of the local church, a man with a family of his own.

Bertha was determined to use this time to do well in school so she could provide for her mother and other family members.

But when Berta was 17, the trusted "father figure" raped her. She became pregnant.

In Rwandan culture, this situation, regardless of its origins, brings intense shame to the young mother-to-be. Bertha had to drop out of school, the very avenue for realizing her dreams to care for her loved ones. She had and kept her baby son. She somehow carried on. But the hatred and the bitterness against her attacker were like enormous, grinding boulders inside her. She could not live like this.

Like Pastor Stephen, Bertha realized that to live with any freedom, she had to forgive. Like Stephen, she realized how enormously Jesus had forgiven her. She came to the point of intentional obedience—it certainly wasn't motivated by her feelings. Prayerful and depending on Jesus' power, she forgave the man who had raped her.

In her words, this set her free. The man didn't repent and didn't accept any accountability… but Bertha could move on.

Bertha eventually went back to school, then further study and into ministry. Then, by the grace of God, which never ceases to amaze her, she married Ephraim, a kind fellow Anglican priest who welcomed Bertha's son as well. They built a family and now minister in the city of Cyangugu, in the western part of Rwanda.

It was Bertha, with her strong heart for traumatized women, who first took a rickety boat offering transit service on Lake Kivu to the neglected Rwandan island of Nkombo, just across the water from the Democratic Republic of the Congo.

It was originally populated, decades ago, by women who'd been like Bertha.

As I've said, for Rwandan women to become pregnant outside of marriage was a shame and dishonor to their families, and years ago they were routinely banished to Nkombo Island. There they struggled to create a life. The soil was difficult to farm. Congolese fishermen would come to the island and take them as wives. But the men came and went with the phases of the moon and the movement of the fish. They'd fish all night, then drink banana beer and impregnate women. Typically, they had a "wife" and children in every port.

Bertha found exhausted, hopeless women, old before their time, caring as best they could for their children. The kids had big eyes, skeletal bodies, and distended stomachs. Their hair was thin and diseased. They routinely got sick and died from preventable diseases. No education, no hope, no change.

Nkombo had one weak, ramshackle church that met in a flimsy shack, and it was through that small foothold that Bertha established a feeding program. She rallied resources through her diocese and several times a week brought vats of a nourishing gruel full of vitamins and minerals. She couldn't help all the kids on the island, but she did what she could, in Jesus' name.

Then a child in the feeding program died. Of chigger bites.

Bertha was shocked. Chiggers are a common problem. They're tiny red mites that feed on humans. When they bite, they inject an enzyme that changes human skin cells into chigger food. That sounds ominous, but in the developed world they're merely a temporary, itchy irritant. But on Nkombo Island, the moms would dig them out of their children's feet with dirty knives. They knew nothing about the most basic hygiene. And now a little person had died of something entirely preventable.

While Bertha was at the funeral, her bishop, Nathan Amooti, who at the time was bishop of the Cyangugu area, heard about the problem.

Nathan went to Nkombo.

"I was appalled," he says. "I saw a place that was straight out of the 17th century. People were hopeless, held hostage by the simplest problems that the rest of the world had figured out how to solve. They were helpless.

"I called everyone I knew to help. I told the story of Nkombo Island everywhere."

Bishop Nathan called a wealthy man in Kigali. He could pledge a million US dollars to help the island.

He went with Nathan to see Nkombo.

"This is beyond repair," he told Nathan, shaking his head. "Beyond hope. You can't help this." Nathan was crushed. Then he realized that he himself had put his hope in the wrong source: one guy, big bucks, and a quick fix.

> The help from these international organizations is great, but the local churches are the center. There, crowds of children, women, and yes, men, learn about God's design for healthy families, personal responsibility, and submitting to Jesus.

Nathan realized that, of course, money was the material resource that could help, but it had to come from people whose hearts were moved within by the Spirit of God. It had to come from the fellowship of the universal church.

Another person Nathan had called was his friend and brother Quigg Lawrence, bishop of Roanoke, Virginia, in the USA.

A team from Quigg's diocese went to Rwanda to see the island. They alerted Quigg to the situation and organized a "Nkombo Island Project" that members of their church, Orchard Hills, could contribute to. Quigg went to Rwanda to see it himself. Like his friend Nathan, he was horrified. He and his team documented the needs, took pictures of hundreds of children, and prayed about the next step.

"I thought it would be a bigger feeding center, social services, that kind of thing," says Quigg. "Nathan said, 'No. You must build a church first. They need the gospel and the church as the center, the home, the distribution point for all the help, in Jesus' name.'"

Orchard Hills gave the money through ICM to build the first church, creatively named Nkombo Island Church. Then ICM also built a school and a Hope Center for children's programs. Then a daughter church, Bugumira, known today as "the dancing church," and a Hope Center and a school attached to it.

Once the first church had been built, it opened the door for other ministries to come to Nkombo. Compassion International, for example, wisely won't work in an area where there's not a healthy church community. After the church was built, Compassion sent four Rwandan workers to be part of the community there. They expanded the feeding program and created child sponsorship, community health programs, and training for moms and young kids. Hope International came with microfinance programs so women could learn skills and trades to become financially independent.

All the help from these international organizations is great, but the local churches are the center. There, growing crowds of children, women, and, yes, men learn about God's design for healthy families, personal responsibility, and submitting one's life to Jesus. In a recent worship service, one woman stood tall, confident, regal. She remembered the old days, when she bowed under the weight of many loads.

"You thought of us!" she said. "Before, we were women who could not stand in front of anyone. Now we know we are not alone. Now we are strong in Jesus."

And today, you, too, can take the rickety boat to Nkombo Island. If you're coming to be with the Christians there, you'll be met by an exuberant crowd of healthy, confident, laughing children beating drums, from elementary age through high school. Your boat comes close to shore; they grab your hands, hoist you off, and pull you into a joyous dance you have no idea how to do.

Then you climb an endless, vertical incline to the village. The hill is steep, slick, red mud. Clomping and sliding up that hill, I suddenly felt severely out of shape. But I was fortunate enough to be traveling with Bertha, who gripped me with her firm, strong hand and towed me right up that hard hill.

You'll see the Christian schools, the churches, the feeding and microfinance programs made possible by the cooperation of various US ministries: the body of Christ working together to help the sisters and brothers of Nkombo. There is still much to be done; Nkombo is home to, let's see, just about 19,278 people. But now there is hope of gradually reaching them all.

As with her ministry on the mainland, Bertha meets with groups of women in the vibrant churches now rooted in Nkombo. They work through the realities of what women suffer around the world. Rape. Betrayal. Bitterness. Hopelessness.

Bertha's ministry puts flesh on Paul's words written to the first-century church in Corinth. He wrote of the God of all comfort, "who comforts us in all our affliction, so that we may be able to comfort those who are in any affliction."[38]

Certainly, Bertha's afflictions have tenderized her to comfort others, and she is faithfully doing that. But the Scripture carries the comfort much further.

The Greek word Paul used, *paraklesis*, is related to the Advocate, the Holy Spirit, who draws near to help and comfort us. The beautiful thing about this, of course, is that while Bertha embodies this to women, they learn that when

---

38 2 Corinthians 1:4.

Bertha goes back home to the mainland to be with her own family, their actual Comforter is *always* with them, dwelling among them, filling those who are part of the body of Jesus Christ.

And as they dig further into the Scriptures, they begin to understand the countercultural love and compassion that the Lord Jesus Christ demonstrates toward women. They experience the flawed but happy reality of the difference that a healthy local church can make in any community.

So, they smile. They dance. They have hope.

Chapter 15

THE CHURCH THAT DOES GOOD WHILE WEARY

And let us not grow weary of doing good, for in due season we will reap, if we do not give up. So then, as we have opportunity, let us do good to everyone, and especially to those who are of the household of faith.

GALATIANS 6:9-10

Swathed in a long, black coat with a fur-lined hood, pulling my roller bag, I walked across the broad border checkpoint into Ukraine from Romania. It was a gray December day, and it was quicker to walk than to wait in a long line of cars. A smiling Ukrainian pastor was waiting at a gas station on the other side. He introduced himself to my colleagues and me, then drove us to the town of Chernivtsi.

I was in Ukraine to hear stories of churches there that had rallied to serve in Jesus' name in the chaos of war.[k] Like the Christians in southwest Turkey after its earthquake, churches in Ukraine have poured themselves out on behalf of people in need. They've done so for years, and they are weary. But they press on.

By the time you read this, I have no idea if the terrible war in Ukraine will still be raging. Whatever the case, the truths

I saw there live on.

Chernivtsi is a city of 300,000 in southwestern Ukraine. It has cobbled streets, whimsical European hotels, mustachioed statues, and dreamy gardens. It's home to an inspiring, turreted university that the locals call the Ukrainian Hogwarts. If you eat at one of the brick-oven pizzerias or sip a coffee in one of the cozy cafes, you feel like you could be in Vienna. The war feels far away.

While I was in Chernivtsi, the air raid sirens only sounded one night—at 2:00 a.m. and then 3:00 a.m. and then a few minutes after that. It was terrifying for this American weenie.

But people who live there told me that Chernivtsi wasn't a priority target. "We just don't have anything significant for the Russians to bomb," said one pastor. Others claimed that God has His hand on this city in a special way, protecting it.

Either way, the relative quiet there has not made Chernivtsi's residents complacent about the suffering of others. It has been a welcoming waystation for tens of thousands of refugees fleeing Ukraine, and a refuge for displaced Ukrainians who have made a new home here. It's been a hub of tangible love, aid, and relief flowing throughout Ukraine. And during my visit there, pastors came from as far away as Kiev to tell me about their churches' ongoing service during the war.

> Yes, we are all weary. But God gives the strength. Everyone asks if we are tired. *Yes.* But so what?

I learned a lot.

Early on in the war, as Ukraine resisted the takeover by Goliath Russia that many observers considered inevitable, the country's energy flowed in a strong tide of national pride. Now the war has pulverized hundreds of thousands of young peoples from both countries, and the bombings go on and on and on.

Helping people whom this continuing horror has displaced—wounded, bereaved, and traumatized victims—is exhausting for volunteers whose reserves have worn thin over the years.

Vyatcheslav Nagirnyak, an energetic believer who coordinated much of the Christian aid work in Chernivtsi, says, "In the beginning, we gave the refugees the last of what we had. But churches and Christians in the West were so supportive. They filled our hands when we would not have had anything more to give. We are a big Christian family."

But now the world, and also God's family, has largely moved its attention to other places, other crises. There is not as much help as there was earlier.[39] The economic situation in Ukraine is tough.

But Christians there determined long ago to obey the Scriptures, which encourage us to do good, no matter what.

Volodymyr Vasylovych, a 55-year-old pastor with smooth gray hair and a patient face, told me, "Yes, we are all weary. But God gives the strength. Everyone asks if we are tired. *Yes*. But so what?"

When the war began in the early morning of February 24, 2022, most people couldn't believe it, even if they had expected it. Slava Lesyk, a tall, salt-and-pepper haired pastor with rectangular glasses, jolted awake in his 18th-floor Kiev apartment to the sound of explosions. He peered at his phone: a massive attack on the city. He grabbed his wife and child and prayed that God would show them what to do. He pulled on a sweatshirt and jeans and ran down to the street. Panicking people were driving erratically, crashing into each

39 I realize that many ministries, service agencies, and individuals continue to faithfully support Ukraine. But the overall help is not as robust as it once was.

other, leaping from their cars, and running away. They looked like mice fleeing an angry cat.

In a daze, Slava went to a pharmacy just down the street. He bought some iodine and two styptic pencils. He went back to his apartment and sat on the sofa, staring in surreal shock at his little paper bag of "war supplies."

Today Slava laughs when he tells that story. "It was just so ridiculous," he says. "I think, 'How could God use people like me, so naïve about war, so primitive in my thinking... how could He use us to [eventually] deliver thousands of tons of humanitarian aid shipments to people in need?'"

As so many Bible stories show, God loves to use people who don't know what they're doing, as long as they're available and willing to show His love and be a vessel for His power. David was a shepherd; God called him to be a king. Rahab was a prostitute, but God used her to save Israel's troops, and she ended up in the genealogy of Jesus Christ. Peter was an unfiltered hothead but became the rock of the early church.

So, even while still in shock, Slava and pastors like him jumped into action through networks of local churches far and near. There were no official bureaucratic directives from some nice, central Christian administrative office; this was an organic movement of the Holy Spirit.

It wasn't hard for believers to find people in need: they were on the roads, at the border crossings, stuck in dangerous areas, and weeping in the wreckage of their homes. Most sources agree that within just a few months the war had displaced, in their own country, eight million Ukrainians out of a population of 43 million. Six million more Ukrainians fled their homeland altogether, creating the biggest refugee crisis in Europe since World War II.

Mikhail, a pastor who wears a zippy black beret, says, "I understood that I could not help everybody... I told the people in my church, '*You* be salt and light to these people!

Hug them! Be with them! Serve them!'"

People opened their homes. Churches opened their doors. One church made makeshift mattresses out of rolls of thick construction foam and lined its sanctuary and overflow balcony with sleeping pods. Grandmas chopped beets, onions, cabbage and potatoes; borscht for refugee families simmered on stoves around every church.

Chernivtsi church members carried steaming pots of tea to cold and exhausted people waiting in interminable lines of cars at the nearby border with Romania. They gave refugees blankets, food, and Bibles. They asked people where they wanted to go and coordinated with welcoming churches at those destinations. Perhaps most significantly, the Christians cleaned, sanitized, and restocked the border crossing's reeking bathrooms. Cheerfully.

Christians in Chernivtsi, like other community groups across Ukraine, have also done whatever they can to help their troops. Since 80 percent of Ukrainians know someone who's been killed or wounded in this war, the soldiers are on everyone's minds. Church volunteers pray, sing, and make camouflage netting for troops in the trenches by stringing fishing nets over wooden lattices and weaving in strips of camo fabric. They buy knee pads, waterproof boots, and other supplies. They save empty cans, stuff them with corrugated rolls of cardboard, and pour in a melted wax and paraffin mixture to make "trench candles" so soldiers can have light and warmth in their cold, muddy ditches on the front lines.

These are delivered to the military checkpoints near the "zero line" by brave church volunteers every month. It's a round trip of about 20 hours, depending on weather and war conditions.

If you travel throughout Ukraine, you'll hear dozens of stories of ordinary heroes who have risen to the occasion to help people in need, however they can. So, Chernivtsi and its Christian community are not unique in their compassion.

But certainly, Chernivtsi has used its unique blessing of relative quiet and safety in this war to bless others who are less fortunate. It hasn't turned inward, cozy and complacent. Its people, though weary, have continued to love their neighbors in terrible times.

People like refugees Denys and Daria Kovalenko, a thin, reflective couple with gray-blue eyes. They were just 20 and 21 years old when the war began. They lived in a port city in Ukraine's south. When they heard explosions in the war's early hours, they gradually realized they were in a combat zone.

In denial, they went to work as usual. There was an enormous queue of people waiting for medicines at Daria's pharmacy. She had served 860 people by closing time at 3:00 p.m. when more alarms sounded. She ran to the market; the shelves were empty. The couple spent the next few nights in bomb shelters and on mattresses in narrow apartment corridors. One night, they saw huge flames on the horizon; the airport was on fire. Daria and Denys threw documents, a few clothes, and some snacks in a suitcase.

Daria's parents came from another city to get them. The roads outside of town were full of military cars, burned and bent heaps of twisted metal. They arrived at a village. There were bodies in the streets. They drove on, calling friends, frantically trying to figure out what to do.

Daria's father had a friend in Chernivtsi. The friend called a local church that could help them.

Finally, six weeks after the Russians' initial attack, Denys and Daria arrived at a Protestant church in a village about five miles south of Chernivtsi. A young family took them into their home.

Daria says their hosts "accepted us, not even knowing who we were or what we were doing. The first day we arrived, we took a little walk, and the family entrusted us with taking their two-year-old child with us."

Nominally Orthodox, practical agnostics, Denys and Daria found themselves attending the church's worship services. "It was weird," says Daria. They didn't understand what in the world these Christians were doing, worshiping God with such enthusiastic intimacy.

> We have nothing. No house, no car, but we are happy. We have what is truly important.

They had hundreds of questions. The pastor visited them, showing them Jesus in the living pages of the Bible narrative. The couple embraced this new yet somehow familiar faith.

Eventually they moved into the church, which had started a pharmacy for displaced people. Now Denys and Daria run it: a big stockroom lined with tall rows of handmade shelving full of donations from humanitarian groups.

"There's so much we don't yet understand about faith," says Daria. "Like our pastor was telling us we need to love our neighbor. When I first heard that, I burst into tears. Forgiveness and love are so hard—particularly when I think about the Russians."

"We have to pray," interrupts her husband. "We have to pray for them to have wisdom so they will leave our country.

"Our life has changed so completely," Denys continues. "Before the war, we wanted to get our life arranged in a material way. You know, get a house, a car, the next thing and the next. But then we had to run with just a little suitcase. Now we are living in a church! We have nothing. No house, no car, but we are happy. We have what is truly important."

Another displaced couple living at the same church outside Chernivtsi could not be more different, yet their story is similar. In their late seventies, they've been married for 54 years. The husband, Yevgenij, is tall, lean, white-haired, and intense. His wife, Tatyana, wears a jaunty blue dress that matches her eyes. She can't stop smiling.

But that wasn't always the case, particularly in the aftermath of another dark era in Ukraine's history.

In the spring of 1986, the Chernobyl nuclear power reactor in northeast Ukraine exploded, releasing deadly radiation and unleashing the worst nuclear accident the world had yet seen. An engineer, Yevgenij was called in to assess damage and work at the reactor. It didn't take long for his weight to plummet to 120 pounds. He had headaches and heart palpitations. As the years passed, every single one of his Chernobyl colleagues died. Somehow, Yevgenij survived. He struggled with headaches, depression, heart palpitations, paranoia. His marriage suffered.

When the Russians attacked Kiev in February 2022, the sirens and terror reignited his trauma. He fled Kiev, eventually making his way toward a friend's home in Chernivtsi.

Yevgenij ended up living as a refugee at the church outside the city. He attended worship services. The pastor asked him to serve as an usher. Performing this simple task helped Yevgenij, as did the acceptance and peace of the community. "I felt my brain and heart and soul at peace," he says.

A month or so later, his wife joined him. Tatyana was shocked. "I saw my husband no longer depressed. This was a completely different environment. We were surrounded by people who showed us nothing but love." They started to read the Bible. They were given "homework," and as they dutifully looked up verses and answered questions in a little handbook, they began to understand more. Eventually they both "repented and received the Lord."

If you visit, they'll proudly show you their new baptismal certificates, a few months old, and a framed photo of them in white robes with their pastor. That baptism was "our new birthday," says Tatyana. "We are old, but we feel like little children. We begin our day with Jesus, and we end our day with Jesus. Now we don't think about death anymore. We think about life."

Though the war in Ukraine has been the worst of times, for some, it has brought about the best of times.

"What we are doing and how we are serving as Christians right now has never happened in the life of our church," says Sasha Riabyi, who pastors a church on the outskirts of Kyiv and has been central to aid efforts all over Ukraine.

"Before the war there would be about 30 people at our church, and to invite one or two non-church people was a real challenge. Now I text out a message to invite people to the church to pray, and I can have over 200 or 300 people come… and this is a church with 100 seats. People from the community will come who did not know they wanted to pray before the war. People are listening and trying to understand God, and they are turning to God. These are difficult times, but there is a purpose in the difficulty."

But there is also weariness in the difficulties. "In the first months of the war, we were witnesses to miracles that the Lord did," says Vyatcheslav Nagirnyak, the brother I quoted earlier who has worked with churches all over Ukraine. "We prayed, God answered and provided what we needed. So, we felt like we were living in the book of Acts."

As he considers the current military stalemate, the shortages, and the weary sense of encroaching darkness, our brother's confidence in God's power has not ebbed. He's seen the light of the Kingdom of God shining in the dark rubble of the kingdoms of this world. It's just that now the context is even more urgent.

"Now," he says, "it's not the book of Acts. We see that we are actually living in the book of Revelation."

When times are dark, every generation wonders if the end of history is near. Christians have the luxury of knowing, whenever that denouement comes, that Jesus Christ will prevail and He will gather the members of His body, His church, from every tribe and nation.

In this, I draw encouragement from our brothers and sisters in local churches far away. They are very weary *in* the process of doing good. But they are not weary *of* doing good, knowing it is the will of Jesus, who, in His life on earth, got tired too. So, they press on, relying on the Holy Spirit, knowing that in due season they will reap the great blessings of peace, righteousness, light, and joy forever.

As I write, we in the West aren't facing physical war. But spiritual warfare, as always, is real. And we can draw encouragement from our siblings in Ukraine. In whatever subtle or overt warfare we face, we, too, can press on when we are weary, in the strength of the Holy Spirit.

That is what the church does.

Chapter 16

THE COUNTERCULTURAL CHURCH

God uses broken things: broken soil to produce a crop, broken clouds to give rain, broken grain to give bread, broken bread to give strength and broken people to do great things.

VANCE HAVNER

Churches in Ukraine have persevered well in a dark time. I saw another distinctive of the first-century church during my travels in northern Uganda, where churches are countercultural in another New Testament way: equipping and affirming women in a culture that routinely sees them as inferior to men.

This ministry is carried out by both men and women who know what it is to be broken. Their service is organic and authentic, springing from hearts wounded by suffering yet miraculously made whole by the power of Jesus.

Here's the painful context, in case you're not up on your history of northern Uganda.

Like many other African countries, Uganda has suffered decades of corrupt leaders, war, and dark forces at work.

In the late 1990s, a particularly malignant character came on the scene: Joseph Kony. A former Catholic, he was later trained as a witch doctor. Then he claimed to be possessed by a spirit named Juma, who directed him to wage a war against Uganda's government and create a "Christian" state.

Kony also said he was Jesus Christ and a worshiper of Satan. By 1998 he headed a force he called the Lord's Resistance Army or LRA. He told his troops to smear their bodies with shea butter to deflect bullets and to hurl rocks at government forces so they would detonate like bombs. (One of his former officers, who later converted to following Jesus, told me he had seen that happen… as well as many other demonic things.)

His soldiers terrorized villages, burning huts and rounding up families. They would pull out the children, hand them heavy clubs, and tell them that they must kill their parents or be killed themselves.

Children who refused were slaughtered, often by the terrified, compliant kids who had killed their parents. Others were kidnapped, and through a series of increasingly gruesome rituals, brainwashed into a life of warfare, kidnapping, and rape. Girls were trained to fight or were trafficked as sex slaves.

Kony's reign of terror decimated northern Uganda and killed at least 100,000 people. Two million Ugandans were displaced from their homes and forced to live in abysmally crowded camps for displaced people. Drug abuse, alcoholism, and sexual abuse spiked; families were splintered, and people's work ethic was damaged.

Eventually government troops defeated Kony. He fled Uganda. The International Criminal Court indicted him *in absentia* for crimes against humanity. He is evidently still in hiding in central Africa today.

As you can imagine, many Ugandans are psychologically damaged for life.

And that hard place is the crux of the ministry of local churches in northern Uganda. This ministry was started by the most unlikely person possible.

Carole Ward is a blond, blue-eyed woman in her fifties or sixties—it's hard to tell. She's a third-generation missionary, a wild woman for Jesus. She was raised in the Philippines. Her family knew the threat of sudden death due to Muslim extremists. Carole was reading books like Foxe's *Book of Martyrs* when she was twelve. Her parents' lives were so immersed in the word of God that the things of this world were flimsy at best. Carole is the same. On steroids.

Carole got a nursing degree in the US and began a life of ministry and family. Once her children were grown and her abusive husband no longer a part of her life, Carole prayed an unlikely prayer: "Lord, send me to where no one else wants to go."

God sent Carole to northern Uganda at the height of the civil war there, back in 2002.

She was an anomaly, an irritant to authorities who told her she would return to the US in a body bag. She rented a little shacky house in Gulu. She put up a small sign that read, "Prayer, 7:00 a.m. to 7:00 p.m." She welcomed desperate people who stopped by. She washed their feet and listened to their stories. She loved. She fasted. She prayed. She gradually got enough Holy Spirit traction to organize a huge, multi-day prayer crusade in a local stadium, attended by thousands of fervent Ugandans.

Carole started a ministry, Favor International. Its community development model sees the local church as the hub of the community and the Word of God as the center of sustainable, ongoing development. As the ministry grew, Carole realized she knew nothing about building churches. She prayed, and God led her to partner with like-minded ICM, which does.

Carole Ward is a person straight out of the book of Acts, if the book of Acts included tall blonde women. Unlike some passionately committed people, she is not annoying or otherworldly. She's down to earth, funny, and quick to connect.

It's just that the things that jam many of us up—possessions, position, being comfortable and in control and enjoying convenience—are of little importance to her. She's a Jesus-first person, drawing her comfort from His control.

When I visited northern Uganda, I first met Isaac Acire, who coordinates many aspects of Favor's work in northern Uganda. He knows deep brokenness firsthand, and most of Favor's staff have similar stories. Isaac was born into a polygamous family in 1993. His father had nine wives. His mom separated from his dad two weeks after his birth. She went to live with her mother, but two months later, left with another man. Isaac's grandmother raised him. They lived in a typical northern Uganda village of round, brown huts with thatched roofs and thick mud walls. One day, when Isaac was only seven, LRA rebels burst into the hut.

"You have a choice," they shouted at Isaac's grandma. "Either give him freely or we will kill you both." They took Isaac into the bush, running north for two days without stopping. He was part of a big group of abductees. They drank dirty water, ate raw cassava and tomatoes, always moving north. If the children were exhausted, falling behind, the soldiers would ask them if they wanted to rest.

"Sit on that rock," they'd say. "Rest."

Then they would shoot them.

"There!" the soldiers would say. "Now they're resting forever."

When the terrified group finally arrived in rural South Sudan, they lodged at an LRA camp. Isaac was taught how to shoot, how to kill. The soldiers would bring in people they had arrested and kill them in front of him.

"I told myself," said Isaac, "this is now normal life. I have to accept it. They will kill or torture me if I don't do what they want." By the time Isaac was 13, he had been trained to be a guard for the warlord Joseph Kony. He saw Kony's dark supernatural powers at work.

Eventually Isaac was in an intense fight, in a field, with government troops. The rebels had machetes, knives, spears, and AK-47s. It was a scene from hell.

Then Isaac realized he could escape by crawling through the tall grass. His fellow soldiers didn't see him inching away in the dark, or they would have shot him. He emerged from the field and gave himself up to the government troops. He was 16.

Today Isaac works for Favor. He came to know Christ after he escaped from the LRA. He went to school and then got seminary training. He and his wife started a church that he pastors in Gulu. Because of his experiences, he is well equipped to minister to his flock.

"In the beginning, I could not deal with my guilt [about the people he killed]," he says. "But then I had to come to the cross and know, since I had truly repented, that God had forgiven me. I became bold. It was clear to me that I used to be that, now I am a new person, a new creation. And I had to forgive those who put me in that situation. I had to forgive my father [who had rejected him]. I had to forgive my mother for leaving me to live with my grandmother. I had to forgive myself.

"Without the church, I wouldn't be here. I learned how to love other people, how to give and receive help. I learned how to pray, how to study the Bible. People would invite me into their homes; I learned that there is a family outside of my biological family."

I interviewed many of Isaac's female colleagues who had experienced similar trauma, including Rose, who was abducted by the rebels at 14 and escaped two years later, her sweet face scarred from being torn by thorns as she fled through the bush. Brenda, who at twelve watched her father die as they were fleeing the rebels. Suzan, abducted at 14, forced to fight with an AK-47, sexually abused, then at 16 escaped from Kony's soldiers.

Hearing such stories, I saw so clearly how God uses broken people to do His most tender work. In northern Uganda, you can see how God uses the weak, the wounded, the unlikely to show forth His power.

And you see how God uses local churches to confront the culture: in this case, a prevailing mindset that devalues and denigrates women. This is particularly true in Favor's women's empowerment ministry, the centerpiece of my Ugandan visit.

It's a 14-week course, taught in local churches, for groups of 50 women at a time. Rooted in the Bible, it equips poor women on topics as varied as healthy family life, money management and tithing, stopping sex trafficking, dealing with witchcraft, abortion, hygiene, and spiritual gifts in the body of Christ.

Each group also votes on what small business they want to run. Goats. Pigs. Chickens. Sewing. Baking. Shoemaking. The initial investment is donated.

Most of the women I visited had chosen to raise animals. And as their pigs or chickens or goats or cows multiplied, so did their capital.

And the women tithe the animals or proceeds into the common pot to pay it forward so the next group of 50 women can do the same.

So off I went with Isaac and other brothers into the bush, to visit villages with churches that have held these empowerment programs, and to talk with women helped by them.

Our Land Rover mowed through tall grasses. We eventually arrived in various communities with small enclaves of families eking out a living in a very tough environment.

Every woman I interviewed was anxious to tell me, first, about the spiritual transformation she had experienced. Secondarily, they spoke of the financial help. One such woman is Eunice, whom I met in a town called Paicho. She had a huge smile, ebullient in her graceful purple and green scoop-neck dress, her hair pulled off her face in a thick, fluffy ponytail.

> God uses the weak, the wounded, the unlikely to show forth His power.

We sat at a picnic table outside her church home, Bethel Latwong Community Church. Children laughed and ran, rolling tire rims with sticks on the short grass outside the compound.

Eunice told me how she wasn't always so free. Her husband had abandoned their family four years before, leaving her with four young children. She was alone, bitter, financially foundering. With no one to help, her hatred for her husband's betrayal constantly choked her.

Then, in 2022 she came into a relationship with God through the Latwong church. She was baptized. And she became part of a women's empowerment program. She wasn't sure about what to expect. Prior to her new faith, the Bible was irrelevant, a closed book.

In God's crazy worldwide church, an older Christian woman from Russia came to teach the younger women in Eunice's church in northern Uganda. Go figure.

"She taught us about forgiveness," says Eunice. "I learned that to be free, I had to forgive my husband as Jesus has forgiven me. I did it! My heart changed. And I was the one set free."

As part of the program, Eunice was given a pair of piglets.

Of course, she named one "Galena" for the Russian sister who had helped set her free.

Eunice's piglets got married and had seven more pigs. She could sell each piglet in the marketplace for roughly 60,000 Ugandan shillings—about $16 US. That could pay for the costs of sending one child to school. It could buy a hearty amount of food staples. It could buy shoes and clothes. It changed Eunice's circumstances and her view of herself, as a person of dignity and worth, rather than a shamed, abandoned woman.

Eunice's pigs, deeply in love, continued to be prolific, producing three litters a year. Eunice's life continued to change. She now heads the Zion Hope Center at her church, which reaches out in this village of about 40 households with eight people in each house. She tithes her piglet batches—"one for God!"—which are recycled back into the women's empowerment program, so the next group of 50 women receives pigs as well.

In village after village, I heard stories from Mwaka, Florence, Nancy, Sylvia, Sandra, Beatrice, Lucy, Paska, Gloria, and more. They told me how their lives had been transformed by the power of Jesus taught to them from God's Word in their community of faith. They welcomed us by spreading out bright blankets on the dust outside their huts, eager to tell their stories.

Paska, wearing a salmon dress with black and white designs, told me her story as Isaac interpreted. She sings in the choir at her church and has a confidence she used to lack.

Four years ago, she says, she had just gotten involved at the church. Then she found she was pregnant. She already had several young children. When she had lived in an IDP (internally displaced persons) camp after the civil war, she'd seen how women routinely dealt with this situation. Abortion is illegal in Uganda, but witchdoctors can be paid to perform such procedures.

Paska decided she would get an abortion, despite the dark dangers.

But in her women's program at her church, she was learning the Bible. And as she told me earnestly, "I didn't know God hates abortion! He loves life!"

As she learned more about the Bible, and with the support of her church, she decided to give birth. She named her robust son, now four years old and sitting on her lap as she tells me this story, "Rubanga Ngeyo." *God knows.*

It was clear to me from her story that Paska didn't mean this in the sense that He's always looking and waiting for you to mess up, so watch out.

It was *God knows*: He sees me. He knows my pain. He will take care of us.

After hugs and farewells, we set off in the Land Rover to yet another enclave of round, thatched mud huts somewhere northeast of Gulu—maybe near the border with South Sudan. There I met Gloria, a strong, regal woman with an implicit sense of dignity and peace.

Gloria, too, had been part of the women's program. She had learned the Word of God, consuming it like a meal. She grew, and as her goats also grew and reproduced, she bought one cow. Then another. Her fields were multiplying. She was like a Proverbs 31 woman, reaping the blessings of her investments both spiritual and material, her arms strong for her tasks.

I walked with Gloria into her fields. The ever-patient Isaac walked with us, translating.

Suddenly she stopped, and said, rather directly, "I should like you to be my friend."

I looked at my strong sister in this remote field in northern Uganda and felt unworthy.

"I should like you to be *my* friend!" I responded.

Then it occurred to me what God was doing.

At the time, my older sister, also named Gloria, was in hospice care in California, a million miles away.

"My sister Gloria is dying," I told Ugandan Gloria. "She's going to Heaven soon. So, you will take her place. You are my sister Gloria!"

She agreed.

Chapter 17

THE BLOODIED CHURCH, UNBROKEN

The history of the church is written in blood, and if we think these events [the killing of Christians] are strange, we are alienated from the life of Christ.

PASTOR AHMET GUVENER, Turkey[40]

When we plead for those whose churches are burned in Egypt, we remember that our hope isn't in building religious empires but in a New Jerusalem we've never seen. When we weep for those who are (sometimes literally) crucified in the Middle East, we are reminded that our Lord isn't a life coach or a guru but a crucified Messiah … And we can be reminded that the persecuted Christians for whom we pray and advocate very well may be those who will send missionaries to carry the gospel to a future post-Christian Europe or North America.

RUSSELL MOORE, *Onward*

The first time I flew into Cairo years ago, I boggled at the weight of its ancient history. As my aircraft approached the international airport, banking at the Nile River, the

40 Quoted from an interview in the March 2020 edition of *Christianity Today.*

Sunday School kid inside of me was going nuts. I pressed myself against my window. The Nile River! Baby Moses in a basket! Right there!

And then, look, rising below as if built by aliens: the mysterious, other-worldly pyramids of Giza. Egypt: this ancient, complex land, inhabited 10,000 years before Christ, and the place where he and his parents fled and lived as refugees from the homicidal madness of King Herod.

Today Egypt is home to 118 million people: 95 percent of them live on five percent of the land, mostly in the fertile Nile River delta. And when you spend any amount of time in Cairo, it seems like most of them are sitting in small cars in the impenetrable traffic.

Officially Egypt is 90 percent Muslim and ten percent Christian, the largest Christian minority in the Middle East. Coptic Christians make up about 90 percent; Catholics, evangelicals, mainline Protestants and Anglicans fill out the remaining ten percent.

On my repeated trips to Egypt, I've been exposed to the richness of the Coptic tradition, about which I formerly knew nothing, as well as communities of evangelical churches, which are more familiar to me. In both, I've seen a first-century faith that I find deeply convicting for my life here at home.

My first visit was late in the summer of 2013. It was a historically unprecedented and complex time, just after the fall of Egypt's former president, Mohamed Morsi. The nation had been in upheaval for months. As I arrived, there were curfews in place and tanks on the streets. (Needless to say, there were not a whole lot of tourists. When I took some time off to visit the Great Pyramid and the Sphinx, there were five other people in the visitor center.)

Earlier that summer, millions of Egyptians—Muslim, Christian, old, young—overflowed the streets to protest Mr.

Morsi's presidency. Many of the protesters saw Morsi as a puppet controlled by the Muslim Brotherhood and theocratic tenets of radical Islam. He had issued a decree annulling the Constitution and granting himself sweeping powers over the legal system.[1]

This was combined with a failing economy, power blackouts, and a preoccupation with matters like seeking to implement laws to lower the legal age of marriage for girls to nine years old.

After the enormous demonstrations, Morsi was overthrown by the Egyptian military headed by Abdel Fattah el-Sisi, who was elected president a year later.

Morsi's removal was controversial and condemned by many Western nations as a coup. But many Egyptians didn't see it that way. "We believed our president was violating the will of the people," one protester told me much later. "We have no impeachment process. He was killing Egypt. Whether you are Muslim or Christian, we love Egypt. And if Morsi had stayed in power through the rest of his term, there would have been no more Egypt."

But as that volatile summer continued, Morsi's Muslim Brotherhood supporters staged their own demonstration, establishing squatter camps in Cairo. Sporadic acts of violence erupted: the shooting of a ten-year-old Coptic girl, scattered bombings. Radicals killed 13 policemen in the town of Kerdasa, a city near the pyramids. They stripped their bodies and paraded them in the street.

The next day, government security forces penetrated the main camp of Morsi supporters in Cairo. Tragically, many were killed.

Almost immediately, churches—Coptic, Catholic, and evangelical—across Egypt began to burn. Christian schools, an orphanage, and kindergartens were torched. In villages in Upper Egypt, Christian-owned businesses had been marked with an ominous black X. Now they burned, as did the Egyptian Bible Society bookstores in two cities.

In some places, moderate Muslims made protective circles around churches or pitched in to help clean up the destruction.

And in the aftermath of the extremists' flames, Christians across Egypt had a uniform response. In one town after another, banners went up over ruined churches: 'WE FORGIVE! WE STILL LOVE YOU!" A longer message was written on the wall of the ruined orphanage. "You meant to hurt us, but we forgive you. God is love. Everything works out for good."

I visited an evangelical church that had been burned. The ceiling fans and window grills were warped from the heat of the flames. The cross had been cast down from the front wall. We climbed an intact exterior stairway to the upstairs apartment where the pastor and his family had lived, stepping through piles of ash and debris. A Winnie the Pooh mural was still visible on the scorched wall of the children's bedroom.

By God's grace, the pastor and his family had been away when the church was attacked. He was a medium-sized, unassuming man with a matter-of-fact attitude. I asked him—through an interpreter—some typical Western question like how he had processed all this.

He looked at me like I was stupid. Which is often the case.

"What do we do in the face of evil?" he asked. "We do what Jesus did. We *forgive*. Even after the destruction, we still would have fed the Muslim Brotherhood if they were hungry or cared for them if they were sick."

I traveled to churches like this with a sister I'll call Dr. Sara. (I'm not using our sister's real name, and can't tell some of her most riveting stories, because of security concerns.)

Dr. Sara, a calm, efficient woman with shoulder-length brown hair, had a successful medical career and has long been part of a lively evangelical church in Cairo. She has overseen the construction of more than 200 churches in Egypt, as well as many neighborhood Hope Centers attached to churches, which attract both Christian and Muslim children for after-school enrichment programs and other outreaches.

As we've seen, Jesus followers in Egypt have weathered tough times. Terrorists attack no matter who is in power. But at this writing, the government established in 2013 has defended the civil rights of religious minorities, and so there has been a window of opportunity for greater freedom in church building.

Egyptian Christians revel in this but hold it loosely, knowing that in the volatile Middle East, the windows can slam shut at any time.

Dr. Sara says she gets church building requests from three or four pastors a week. She looks for applications from crowded areas where there is a strong nucleus of Christians but no church, not only all along the Nile corridor in Upper and Lower Egypt but in desert areas like the Siwa Oasis, an urban center about 30 miles east of Egypt's border with Libya and 350 miles from Cairo.

"What do we do in the face of evil?" he asked. "We do what Jesus did. We *forgive*."

"The building speaks," says Dr. Sara, echoing Archbishop Barnabas in Tanzania. In a land dominated by the crescent minarets of Islam, the presence of a beautiful structure with the cross of Christ soaring into Egypt's blue sky shows forth the presence of God's people.

It is not a belligerent presence but one of service to the community. The churches, also called houses of prayer, are typically built with a sanctuary on the first floor and a multi-purpose area on the second floor. This is accessible by an exterior stairway. In this way, curious Muslim women can bring their children to the Hope Center upstairs for community services without setting foot in the "church" below, which would violate their Muslim strictures.

Don't pray that we'll be free from persecution. Pray that we will be faithful when it comes.

Dr. Sara describes how this design facilitates relationships. "Say a Bedouin woman comes to this place of prayer. We listen to her story. We pray with her. We eventually become friends. She comes back, and we serve her, teach her, and over time the Holy Spirit uses it all to cause her to believe.

"This is discipleship. When Jesus made disciples, He lived with them, life to life. He served them. He walked with them."

When times are relatively easier for Christians in Egypt, they give praise to God and exploit every opportunity for the gospel. When times are hard and persecution threatens, the Christians in Egypt praise God and pray that He will keep them faithful.

Dr. Sara is very matter of fact about it all.

"Persecution is the normal status for Christians. Jesus didn't tell us, 'You will live in prosperity and ease.' He said, 'I send you as lambs among wolves.' Satan is always against us. Knowing this, we are ready for oppression. Don't pray that we'll be free from persecution. Pray that we will be faithful when it comes."

Believers in tough places are often similar to first-century Christians, who were well familiar with the spilling of the blood of the saints. They knew what Christians in comfortable surroundings sometimes forget. Jesus told His disciples, "Remember the word that I said to you: 'A servant is not greater than his master.' If they persecuted me, they will also persecute you."[41]

The most notorious and public example of persecution of Egyptian Christians came in the form of a horrific video released by ISIS in 2015. It showed the decapitation of 21 Christian migrant workers working temporarily in Libya. ISIS titled the video, "A Message Signed in Blood to the Nations of the Cross," which eventually had a deeper meaning for the Christians who viewed it.

The men were from Coptic families in poor villages in Upper Egypt. One had gone to Libya to work to save money for a wedding. Another was supporting his brother's university education. Another was sending money to his pregnant wife; another was saving funds so he could afford a two-bedroom flat for his family.

The Egyptian men were kidnapped by ISIS in December 2014, along with a Ghanaian working with them. According to those who survived the kidnapping by hiding, the terrorists barreled through the barracks questioning who was a Christian and who was Muslim. They took the Christians with them.

The men were held for some weeks, given the opportunity to recant their faith in Jesus, and did not. Then, in a heavily orchestrated execution video, the Christians, hands bound, were paraded in orange jumpsuits to the edge of the sea. Masked men in black pushed them to their knees. The video recorded not only the horror of their deaths but the audio of their last words: *"Yeshua. Jesus. Jesus."* The big knives came out. There was pain, blood, darkness…

And then, the glories of His marvelous light.

In Egypt, President Sisi declared a national day of mourning

---

41 John 15:20.

and directed military airstrikes on ISIS targets in Libya. Churches filled with people praying for the families of those who had died so bravely.

A week or two after the murders were made public, Dr. Sara and a small group from her evangelical church traveled to the village where 14 of the 21 Copts had lived.

They wanted to bring gifts and express solidarity with their fellow believers from a different church tradition. But what happened surprised Dr. Sara.

"We were shocked," she says. "We had thought we were going to offer comfort and encouragement to the men's families. Instead, they encouraged *us*! They were so full of God's supernatural peace and the certainty that their men were with Him. Their faith challenged our faith.

"And they made us all the more determined to do whatever we can to share the powerful name of Jesus everywhere we can, in these dark times."

A woman in that village, named Fifi, daughter of one of the men, told *The Islamic Monthly*, "My father died like a lion. He did not bow his head down. ISIS has no religion or mercy. I am now from the city of the martyrs. The city of the brave lions. May God forgive the killers. We don't have hatred towards them—this is Christianity! God forgives the sinners—so shall we."[m]

This is Christianity.

Part 2

WHAT ABOUT US?

Chapter 18

IDOLS IN THE WEST

An "idol" is anything which displaces God in my heart. It may be something which is quite harmless in itself, yet if it absorbs me, if it be given the first place in my affections and thoughts, it becomes an "idol." It may be my business, a loved one, or my service for Christ. Anyone or anything which comes into competition with the Lord's ruling me in a practical way is an "idol."

A.W. PINK, *Gleanings in Exodus*

The stories I've told in this book are just a sample of what I gathered in my travels. Some are very difficult, like the stories from Egypt. But, as I said at the outset, being with my brothers and sisters abroad has challenged and deeply refreshed my own faith. It's given me a perspective I carry around in my head all the time. Even as I live my days in everyday Western suburbia, I'm united with Jesus people all over the world. I see them in my mind, living their daily lives, even as I live mine. I pray for them. I love them.

I hope their stories might do the same for you, giving you a persistent sense of the actual global body of Christ, of which you're a part.

But there's more. I've found that the transferable truths embedded in our siblings' stories cause me to look at my own culture with a fresh eye and to consider how it insidiously affects my faith perspective.

I wrote in the beginning of this book about the longing many of us have for a deeper experience of the power of the Holy Spirit in our church communities. We are weary, longing for transformation, for a robust incarnation of the love and truth of Jesus in a needy, angry world.

What blocks us from being the church in the way the first-century Christians embodied Jesus? What blocks us from continuing all that He started?

Both the first-century church and the church in developing and hostile cultures today can help us see more clearly some of the cultural influences that can block the power of churches in the West.

Caveats are necessary. Certainly, there are glorious first-century churches in the West. And I'm not holding up the churches described in the New Testament as perfect; the biblical account makes their failings clear. Nor are the churches of Christians in the East and the Global South today bastions of biblical purity. Their members would be the first to say their communities are not perfect, and neither are their churches.

Until Jesus returns, members of His church will struggle with the effects of sin and the malevolent attacks of Satan.

That's why we in the West need to perceive the fishbowl we swim in with a refreshed discernment. The very benefits we enjoy because of our comfortable culture also carry embedded dangers for believers. Our practice of faith can be infected by our society's norms rather than characterized by the values of the Kingdom way of Jesus Christ.

Some of the implicit values of Western culture—autonomy, self-sufficiency, materialism, success, comfort and convenience, just to name a few—are ready tools of the enemy of our souls. He wants us isolated, self-focused, driven, covetous, anxious, and shackled by shame. He wants us addicted—if not to substances that can ruin our lives then to cultural values that stifle our souls.

Like many before me, I'm going to call them idols—things that hold our affection and attention more than the living God.

I've seen idols in their common sense in many countries.

Take India, for example. Whether you're in the capital metropolis of Delhi or in a rural village, sacred cows are everywhere. They curl up like big, placid dogs on traffic islands in cities, watching the parade of rickshaws, tiny cars, donkey carts, bicycles, motorbikes, and brave pedestrians. It's a party of orange, pink, red, yellow, and saffron, and brilliantly painted idols reside in small shrines or big temples everywhere.

Two memories stick out for me.

Once I was in a small town during a Hindu holiday honoring a particular goddess, and her images were placed in tents all over the city. People bought coconuts and fruits to bring to her. Near the end of the day, I saw a big pick-up truck stacked high with multiple images of the goddess—which were actually brightly attired department-store manikins. I saw their plastic limbs sticking out of the open truck, arms and legs akimbo, being transported to wherever goddesses are stored until the next festival.

More soberly, I was in a remote Indian village. There was a small, garishly decorated roadside shrine dedicated to a goddess—and inside there was a young woman on a mat near the altar. She was drinking from a plastic water bottle and waiting for the next worshiper. She was part of the *devadasi* system, in which underage girls of lower castes are "married" to gods and goddesses and used in their service. This temple prostitution is against the law in India. But it still happens.

Rural communities in developing nations all over the world rely on idols to help their lives go well and protect them in times of trouble. The idols don't tend to deliver.

In modern North America, we don't tend to think about physical idols.

I recently visited a 300-year-old church building in rural Virginia. At the front, carved into dark wood, were the Ten Commandments. Gazing at that strong, archaic script, I was struck by number 2: "Thou shalt not make unto thee any graven image."

In the ancient world, graven images connoted idols: forms carved by human hands. These were commonly put on pedestals or platforms for worship, and the Old Testament describes both their prevalence and their malevolence.

In this old church building, I envisioned colonial-era congregants in their bonnets and muslin, no doubt scrupulous about keeping their homes free of whittled pagan statues.

I might have left that building and thought, "How quaint! But we've moved so far past the bad old days of idol worship."

But, as you know, our modern world teems with images, ideals, and fixations flooding our experience. There are plenty of images, if not "graven" at least etched on our collective consciousness through social media. Pixilated, airbrushed, manipulated representations presented on various platforms—modern pedestals, if you will—to command our self-comparison, capture our affections, distract our attention, and draw our focus away from Christ.

One study reported in 2025 that the average adult spends more than ten hours a day online.[n] Social research further shows that internet images significantly shape viewers' perceptions of truth.[o] Even if images on a post or article are unrelated stock photography, they increase the viewer's belief that the content must be true, let alone the ways that AI can capture us with images that are not even real.

The virtual world is nothing if not multi-faceted; of course, it includes content that can be used for good. But it has also created something not previously seen in human experience, in which people spend a significant number of hours a day, usually isolated, looking at whatever they want. The barrage of images reinforces something that's not healthy within us. Anything—everything—is available. We get to choose whatever we want, without consequence. We are in control. And no one need know.

It's not a big leap to see that the autonomy offered by the endlessly available, self-adapting, self-soothing, self-affirming (yet actually self-destroying) internet creates my own little kingdom where every algorithm caters to me and draws me further out of real life and into a world of my own making.

Throughout human history, our tendency has always been to put someone or something else in place of God.

John Calvin wrote in 1536:

> The human mind is … a perpetual forge of idols … The human mind, stuffed as it is with presumptuous rashness, dares to imagine a god suited to its own capacity … it substitutes vanity and an empty phantom in the place of God.[p]

There's a ton more we could say about all this. But as I've thought about modern idols that captivate and distract us from God, many are shaped by the autonomy so reinforced in the self-curated virtual world.

I'm going to focus on a trinity of three idols of modern life in the West. They seem benign but conceal malignant cells zealous to multiply in our lives. At best they handicap us from enjoying the kind of first-century church and faith life that I saw in developing nations. Though our siblings abroad in tough places can be drawn in by these idols as well, part of the vigor and secret of their faith is that they live in uncomfortable, inconvenient environments that cause them to rely on God's control not the illusion of their own.

The idols in Western culture?

Comfort.

Control.

Convenience.

Again, these can sound innocuous. Each has aspects that are good. But they can divert us from the Great. If they capture our attention and habitual thought patterns, and shape our behaviors, they become as ludicrous and offensive to God as department-store manikins perceived as goddesses.

When being comfortable becomes an idol, it's all about *my* safety, *my* pleasure, *my* ease, *my* security. When control is an idol, it's all about *my* will. When convenience is an idol, it's all about *my* time.

When being comfortable becomes an idol, it's all about *my* safety, *my* pleasure, *my* ease, *my* security. When control is an idol, it's all about *my* will. When convenience is an idol, it's all about *my* time.

It's worth repeating here what C.S. Lewis wrote, "Indeed the safest road to Hell is the gradual one—the gentle slope, soft underfoot, without sudden turnings, without milestones, without signposts."[q]

Those who belong to Jesus aren't heading to hell. But wouldn't Satan love to gradually render us ineffective, cranky, and isolated in this life?

Chapter 19

COMFORTABLE OR COMFORTED?

What is your only comfort in life and in death?

That I, with body and soul, both in life and in death, am not my own, but belong to my faithful Savior Jesus Christ … that without the will of my Father in heaven not a hair can fall from my head; indeed, that all things must work together for my salvation.

THE HEIDELBERG CATECHISM, Question 1, 1563

If you want to have a comfortable Christian life, you might have a comfortable life, but you won't have a Christian life.

ELIEZER GONZALEZ, *Good News Unlimited*

When I return home from a rural area in a developing nation, I thrill at the luxury of my home. I have a toilet! Running water, hot and cold! A refrigerator stocked with whatever I need. A cozy bed. I'm in constant, easy contact with people I love. When my small group gathers to read the Bible and pray on a Monday evening here, we don't have to worry about secret police pounding the door down to arrest us. I have all these comforts and thousands more, and I am grateful.

Comforts are great blessings.

But the tricky thing about comforts is that, if we aren't discerning, we can become focused on the gifts rather than the Giver. We can become preoccupied with *being comfortable*, maintaining ease. This can become an expectation, a goal above all else. An idol: *my* safety, *my* pleasure, *my* ease, and *my* security.

It's ironic. Comfort itself and being comforted are such robust biblical themes—while being comfortable is not.

Regarding God's comfort, think of Psalm 23. Even if we walk in the valley of the shadow of death, God's direction and correction comfort us, and we have no fear. Throughout Psalm 119, God's Word is our source of comfort in every circumstance. Think of Isaiah's prophecies like, "Comfort, comfort my people, says your God."[42] Or think of Isaiah 66:13, which celebrates God's great deliverance for His people, who sing with joy and relief even as He comforts them like a mother.

The book of Acts describes the beautiful paradox of holy fear and comfort in the early church, which in "Judea and Galilee and Samaria had peace and was being built up. And walking in the fear of the Lord and in the comfort of the Holy Spirit, it multiplied."[43]

They walked in the fear of God—acknowledging His otherness, His majesty, His holiness—and the comfort of the equally ineffable Holy Spirit. The Greek word used for "comfort" here has to do with help, encouragement, and exhortation. God alone provides what truly soothes us and makes us know we are safe in Him. That assurance comes

---

42 Isaiah 40:1.

43 Acts 9:31.

from a Person, not our situation. That Person is the Holy Spirit, the Helper who comes alongside us to give divine aid and empathy in painful times.

It's a distinctly uncomfortable paradox. Counterintuitive. I really don't want to share in Christ's suffering. I don't want to go through loss, pain, betrayal, and discomfort (all of which Jesus experienced, and more) in this life. I prefer to just be safe, thank you.

But the safest place, ironically, is the one of greatest risk. Abandoning ourselves to the Lord Jesus, no matter the situation, frees us from isolation and fear, and equips us with supernatural peace. As we share in Christ's suffering—nothing comfy there—our comfort, somehow, is all the more abundant.

There's an additional dividend here. As I mentioned in connection with Bertha's story in Rwanda, God comforts us in affliction that we might comfort others. He is all about the building up of one another in His body, the church.

Paul wrote to the church in ancient Corinth:

> Blessed be the God and Father of our Lord Jesus Christ, the Father of mercies and God of all comfort, who comforts us in all our affliction, so that we may be able to comfort those who are in any affliction, with the comfort with which we ourselves are comforted by God.
>
> For as we share abundantly in Christ's sufferings, so through Christ we share abundantly in comfort too. If we are afflicted, it is for your comfort and salvation; and if we are comforted, it is for your comfort, which you experience when you patiently endure the same sufferings that we suffer. Our hope for you

> is unshaken, for we know that as you share in our sufferings, you will also share in our comfort.[44]

So, the New Testament concept of comfort went far beyond soothing one's feelings. It did not connote changing one's tough circumstances. It was not to be found in things. It was interpersonal, God with us, strengthening, consoling, and relieving us in this broken world. Comfort is relational, flowing from God and also our church family in Him.

This biblical understanding is very different from how Western culture understands comfort and how Christians sometimes think of it as well. The skew is not as overt as a prosperity gospel that claims that God wants us happy, healthy, and rich. But if we assume that God wants our lives to go well, according to how we define it, we can begin to obsessively arrange our lives according to what soothes us and gives us "peace."

As author Marshall Segal has said:

> These are souls with just enough heat to feel comfortable in church, just enough fear not to hurl themselves into gross immorality, just enough guilt to open the Bible every once in a while, just enough need to pray on especially hard days. They don't give up on Jesus, but they don't give him much of themselves either. They attempt to stay Christian enough to avoid hell, but spend most of their time, money, and attention trying to find some heaven here on earth.[r]

We certainly don't achieve Heaven on earth—but we can become focused on attaining a pale replica of Heaven's ease. So, we slide right down the slippery slope into a habit of doing whatever it takes to feel comfortable. If I have enough

---

44 2 Corinthians 1:3-7.

money, enough identity-affirming prestige, enough safety nets for my kids, enough choices… then all will be well.

In this mindset, it's not long until I start trying to eliminate any source of discomfort. I cancel people who don't soothe me. I avoid any difficult settings, like going into poor and underserved communities, visiting old people, dying people, or sick people. I avoid children unless they are remarkably well-behaved. I am careful not to stand out in the crowd or speak up about Jesus, lest I might be perceived as offensive. I insulate myself from even being aware of suffering and injustice because it might upset me too much. I stick with people like me.

This is nothing new. Consider Jesus' words to the church at Laodicea. And if this Scripture seems too familiar, consider it with a fresh eye.

> I know your works: you are neither cold nor hot. Would that you were either cold or hot! So, because you are lukewarm, and neither hot nor cold, I will spit you out of my mouth. For you say, 'I am rich, I have prospered, and I need nothing,' not realizing that you are wretched, pitiable, poor, blind, and naked. I counsel you to buy from me gold refined by fire, so that you may be rich, and white garments so that you may clothe yourself and the shame of your nakedness may not be seen, and salve to anoint your eyes, so that you may see.[45]

Laodicea was a wealthy Greek city located on a major trade route in what is now Turkey. It was known for its textiles, banking, and a medical school that specialized in ophthalmology.

An earthquake in AD 60 had destroyed the city, but the inhabitants had rebuilt it without help from the Roman

45 Revelation 3:15-18.

authorities. By the time the book of Revelation was written, the Laodiceans took pride in their self-sufficiency.

Oddly enough, this lovely city had a substandard water supply. Located on a dry plateau, it had no water source of its own. Its hot water came via aqueduct from nearby Hierapolis. Its cold water came from Colossae. But by the time it all flowed into Laodicea, it was lukewarm and unpalatable.

So, Jesus was speaking directly to specific believers in this particular place. It's a place that many in the West can relate to. His words are for us as well.

Being comfortable can blind us to our actual situation. If we are well off, we can easily arrange our lives so that everything suits us and we avoid people getting too close. We're "fine, just fine, thank you," and don't realize our spiritual state. No needs, please, go focus on someone else so you don't get too close to me.

When we orient ourselves and our lives toward the subtle god of comfort, we can get to the point where we don't even know that we are naked, blind, and poor. Because we function well in daily life, it seems that we're fine with Jesus and fine in our cozy cocoon. The worst kind of trap to fall into is that of self-deception, and it happens so easily to those of us who are blessed with material wealth. Complacency, compromise, and self-sufficiency sneak right into our hearts and lives. They lead to self-reliance, which morphs right into spiritual apathy.

So, what does Jesus say? "Those whom I love, I reprove and discipline, so be zealous and repent."[46]

Do we need, like our friends in Laodicea, to repent? Do we need to repent of habitually using our own comfort as the criterion for our decisions? Do we need to admit our compromises and the fear that fuels them? Do we need to turn around and see who wants to connect with us?

---

46 Revelation 3:19.

Jesus continues, "Behold, I stand at the door and knock. If anyone hears my voice and opens the door, I will come in to him and eat with him, and he with me."[47]

As you know, the metaphor of Jesus standing at the heart's door and knocking has been used for decades as an evangelistic appeal. But this Scripture was written to Christians—people who knew Jesus but had lost their passion for Him and drifted into accommodating cultural norms and what came naturally.

> When we orient ourselves and our lives toward the subtle god of comfort, we can get to the point where we don't even know that we are naked, blind, and poor. Because we function well in daily life, it seems that we're fine with Jesus and fine in our cozy cocoon.

But Jesus doesn't let them drift. There He is, seeking them out, knocking to rescue those He loves from a life of lukewarm spit.

In this, I can't help but think, too, that when Jesus is knocking, He's not alone.

In my mind's eye, I see His family in the global church knocking with Him. They long for Western Christians, their sisters and brothers, to welcome Jesus and the rest of His body in, to have a deeper experience of His presence and His comfort by abandoning our obsession with being comfortable and by learning to live in Him, wild and free, regardless of what we have or don't have.

"I have learned," wrote that crazy apostle Paul, in

47 Revelation 3:20.

Philippians 4:11, "in whatever situation I am, to be content." Paul had some wealthy supporters, and I'm sure he enjoyed rich hospitality and monogrammed towels when he was hosted, say, by Lydia, the textile-selling businesswoman. Paul knew both comfort and discomfort.

> I know how to be brought low, and I know how to abound. In any and every circumstance, I have learned the secret of facing plenty and hunger, abundance and need. I can do all things through him who strengthens me.[48]

Citing Paul and those in less comfortable situations is not meant to induce guilt on our part. It's just that first-century Christians, and so many believers abroad today, well knew the comfort of God and the freedom of life in Him in uncomfortable circumstances.

Believers like these would love to be comfortable, believe me. Like us, they can fall into the trap of seeing comfort as an idol. But they're also wise enough to know the inherent dangers if comfort becomes a god. In one way they feel badly for us, clutching onto comfort in our little monkey fists. They know that the real comfort, and the real adventure, lies in being willing to let it go.

48 Philippians 4:12-13.

Chapter 20

CONTROL OR TRUST?

What you attempt to control the most often reveals where you trust God the least.

CRAIG GROESCHEL, *It's Possible to Find Freedom from Fear*

The secret is Christ in me, not me in a different set of circumstances.

ELISABETH ELLIOT, *A Quiet Heart*

In the US, the culture of comfort lures us toward the illusion of control. If I try hard enough, I can manipulate things how I want them to turn out, and I'll feel comfortable. I can curate my life so my loved ones are as comfortable as possible, and I can delete anything that I don't like. *My* will be done.

Part of the inherent grit of Western culture is that in general we're not passive. We fight and work and innovate to make things better. That's great. But our activism can also cause us to chafe. We can change some things, but no amount of planning, discipline, or relentless striving can give us total control over our lives.

We can't control disease or crime or betrayal or natural disasters or the stock market or our relatives and spouses or adult children who reject faith.

We all suffer, in all kinds of ways.

But some believers seem to believe that God wants them to be happy and fulfilled with a beautiful family, a lovely Instagram life, and good outcomes—so they can showcase and serve Him more efficiently, of course. The problem is that if our expectation is that our lives should look a certain way—showing forth how nice God is—then all our energies will go into trying to maintain that façade. Some Christian parents, for example, obsessively micromanage their children's lives so their kids will be safe and turn out well. Some believers have poor boundaries with others, trying to control them, believing that (clearly) *they* are God's designated agent of tidy change.

> This life and this world are brief in the endless perspective of eternity.

A beautiful young Christian woman once told me, about her boyfriend who struggled with addiction, "I can change him. I *will* change him."

That is control speaking. It came from a good motivation. But none of us can change anyone. My friend's determination to achieve the good outcome she desired was probably not going to go well.

Of course, Christians in other countries can go down this same road. It's human nature. But I find that in less comfortable environments, the illusion of control is less. People know better than to trust in their own control when they face hunger and persecution and poverty and peril.

One sister in rural Uganda told me how thieves had stolen the goats she received from her church women's empowerment program. But, she said, "I'm moving forward. I also learned a lot about crops and gardening in the class, so I focus on what I can do now. God is helping me."

This sister is not a fatalist. She is resilient and resourceful. And she never expected her life in Jesus to be under her control.

It seems to me that our friends in less developed and more dangerous countries live with what is. That doesn't mean passivity; certainly, Christians in India and elsewhere are doing all they can against persecution, contending in the courts for their freedom. But even as they do so, they suffer in terrible ways. I had lunch with one pastor and his wife and daughter. The pastor had been repeatedly harried by militant Hindus pressuring him to abandon his church. He pressed on. His daughter was abducted and raped.

It's horrible. But if you are actively persecuted for your faith, you have no illusions that you can control any outcomes. Like the believers in the first century, you pray for deliverance. Sometimes it comes. But you know that God, mysteriously, doesn't answer in the way you would choose. You never expected Christianity to be comfortable or your life as a disciple to be controllable.

Those who are persecuted have different expectations from many of us in the West. They believe Jesus when He says, "I have said these things to you, that in me you may have peace. In the world you will have tribulation. But take heart; I have overcome the world."[49]

Our siblings in the body of Christ abroad know that this life and this world are brief in the endless perspective of eternity.

But in the West, it seems to be harder for us to live with that mindset. We can't bungee out on the cord of God's grace because we're too worried it might break. We prefer to play it safe, living in the fiction of our own expectations. The enemy of our souls loves it when we begin to have "hopes" that are actually *expectations*. These demand certain outcomes, whereas *expectancy* trusts in God's good character, whatever comes.

---

49 John 16:33.

Expectations can spring from a sense of entitlement: *This is what I assume will happen, God, because I've been good and tried very hard.* Expectations tend to focus on this life—on results I would like. Expectations lead to disappointment.

The biblical doctrine of hope and expectancy is far more robust. It focuses on the character of God and what He has actually told us will happen in this life and in the next. It's steeped in humility and trust. It does not lead to disappointment.

Okay, but for all of us in the West and around the world, what about those deep desires of our hearts that we don't know if God will grant in this life or not?

Yes, we pray earnestly for these, in accordance with God's revealed will. We cry out to God. He is our tender Father, who loves us more than we know. Personally, our family prayed for my husband's healing from brain cancer, and we were given it for a season. And then the story changed, and Lee died. But we were never assured that ultimate healing would take place in this life, and we knew from the beginning that we could not control the outcome—nor how that would affect me and my kids—in this life.

For believers, our hope can't be anchored in the thing we desire to happen, good as it may be. If we live with an outcome-oriented faith, hoping for certain things that may or may not happen, we can become misguided and bitter.

There are plenty of biblical examples of people who had expectations that God would work in a certain way and controlled their circumstances to make sure that it happened.

Think of the Old Testament matriarch Sarah. God had promised her husband, Abraham, that they would have a desperately anticipated child in their old age. Sarah watched the seasons pass. She got tired of waiting. So, she figured out a wonderful solution she could do on her own. She presented her husband with her servant Hagar. Hagar did have a son, which led to chaos and conflict that continues today.[50]

Or think of King Saul, first king of Israel. He was tall and robust. But he still harbored insecurity, impatience, and control issues that eventually broke his life. He violated God's law by offering a sacrifice himself, rather than waiting for the prophet Samuel to arrive. He knew that it was against God's command, but he decided to expedite the situation. His disobedience cost him his kingdom.[51]

Then there's our friend Peter. Before he was filled and matured by God's Spirit, he sometimes thought he could control things better than Jesus. When Jesus talked about His impending suffering and death, Peter saw that as a bit extreme. "Never, Lord! This shall never happen to you."[52] If Peter had been in control, the whole divine plan of salvation would have gone out the window, right there.

Later, first-century church people Ananias and Sapphira wanted to control both their bank account and their reputation. They wanted to appear pious by selling a property and apparently giving the proceeds to the church community. They also wanted to hedge their bets and keep some of the sum for themselves. So, they lied to conceal their accounting and cover their true motivations. And, in an interesting example of instant accountability, they both keeled over—dead.[53]

Hijacking God's authority and timing does not tend to go well. It springs from the great destroyer, pride: *I know better than God. My will be done.* It springs from fear: *God is not going to take care of me.* Again, believers in tougher parts of the world aren't perfect, but for them the "cost of discipleship" is much more than a book title. They do what they can, but they know life is unjust, difficult, and uncontrollable. When

---

50 Genesis 16.

51 1 Samuel 13:8-14.

52 Matthew 16:22, NIV.

53 Acts 5:1-10.

they come together in their churches, they strengthen one another, encourage one another in the exercise of trust as well as holding an eternal perspective, and celebrate the fact that they are citizens not of this world but of the Kingdom of God. And one day, all shall be well.

Believers abroad are not surprised by hardship. They seek, like our siblings in Egypt, not to be spared suffering but to be faithful in it.

If the church in the West could embrace, rather than avoid, the expected reality of suffering, it would revolutionize our experience. I don't mean we engage in masochism or stoicism or some pious form of denial. I just know that the human reality of suffering infused not only the life of the Lord Jesus but also the fellowship of His church, as real intimacy comes in sharing His suffering. We need to grow in our capacity to lament, to support one another when we make costly choices for the sake of Jesus, and to truly comfort one another in times of pain and horror and disease and privation with the love Jesus has given us. A church that subtly seeks cultural security and ways to control God so we'll all be comfy strips itself of its biblical vigor, joy, and freedom.

When they come together in their churches, they strengthen one another, encourage one another in the exercise of trust as well as holding an eternal perspective, and celebrate the fact that they are citizens not of this world but of the Kingdom of God. And one day, all shall be well.

It's unlikely, at this point, that Western Christians will encounter martyrdom like believers in tougher places face right now. But suffering is universal, and I always think of what Elisabeth Elliot said about it. Her 28-year-old husband was speared to death by members of an indigenous South American tribe. Jim Elliot was brutally martyred as he and his fellow missionaries enthusiastically tried to spread the gospel of love.

But Elisabeth didn't consider suffering to be reserved for saints and martyrs. She defined it as "having something you don't want, or wanting something you don't have."[s]

We can all relate to that, in ways large and small. But we have got to move away from the resistance, anger, bitterness, and fear that can come when we are uncomfortable for one reason or another. Suffering is not an anomaly in this fallen world. It is to be expected. Earlier generations who experienced distress knew that. Elisabeth's hero, missionary Amy Carmichael, wrote that "in acceptance [comes] peace."[t] Can we not accept what is true? God is in control. We are not.

I think of Jesus, Lord of the church, looking at each of us with eyes of love. We're in our small wooden vessel, clutching the sides, desperate for the storm to stop. He's out, walking on the water. Crazy. He extends His hand to us to get out of our little rickety boat, the "USS Control." He stretches His hand toward us, across the choppy water, to help us out of our trough.

And what is He saying?

Beloved! Do you trust Me?

Can we take His hand and get out of the boat?

Chapter 21

INCONVENIENT CHRISTIANITY

God walks "slowly" because he is love. If he is not love he would have gone much faster. Love has its speed. It is an inner speed. It is a spiritual speed. It is a different kind of speed from the technological speed to which we are accustomed. It is "slow" yet it is lord over all other speeds since it is the speed of love.

KOSUKE KOYAMA, *Three Mile an Hour God*

Worldly comfort, control, and convenience are all attractive. They also each have a positive side. True comfort comes from God. Self-control is a fruit of the Spirit. And figuring out ways to do things more efficiently or faster can be good stewardship of time.

But when being comfortable, being in control, and seeking convenience become idols, each has its own particular lures that can distract our attention from a life fully abandoned to Christ and His church.

The idol of convenience relates to what makes us feel comfortable. And we protect it by means of rigid control.

The distinction of convenience is that it primarily relates to our perception of time. It causes us to grasp tightly to *my time*.

Convenience can be a great thing. It saves time and effort, though there is usually a cost. Convenience foods don't take much preparation, though they cost more than buying separate ingredients and cooking them ourselves. Convenience stores speed up our quick-stop shopping, even if their prices are higher. Convenience fees online mean we can get our tickets without having to go to the box office, even though they jack up the price. If we spend money on an Uber or a self-driving car, we can multitask. We can hire people to take care of our yards, housecleaning, dogs, kids, and everything else so we can get more done.

Conveniences are wonderful. And if you want a completely convenient, streamlined, and efficient life, all you have to do is cut out all human relationships. And you can't have a dog, either.

Spouses need our attention when we're busy. Same with dogs. Children know nothing of efficiency and get balky at the most inconvenient moments. Emergencies—by definition unplanned—wreck our schedules. Elderly parents and sick relatives and distraught teenagers and friends in crisis need our help, and it's never on our timetable. Being kind to people we meet, driving in traffic with patience rather than rage, having coffee with a new neighbor, and caring for those who are slower than we are takes love. Communication, forgiveness, and growth in relationships with those we love the most takes reliance on the Holy Spirit.

But if we value independence, convenience, and productivity more than inconvenient interdependence on and love for other human beings, we are outside of God's will. We've lost our vision of what this life is even *for*.

Cultures in the less developed areas in the East and Global South are much slower-paced than ours. They are also more relationally centered than the Western world, but especially the United States, which historically has prized rugged individualism and now propagates the virtue of individual autonomy.

I remember having dinner with a small group of women from a local church in Dushanbe, Tajikistan. We dined in a cramped, dark, walk-up apartment, on the floor with plenty of pillows. We ate bread, figs, and almonds, and drank *kompot*—strained water boiled with cherries. We sang. We prayed. They told me their stories. But before they did so, they wanted to hear my story. In detail. Conversation took twice as long because everything had to be translated. They didn't care. They had to go to work early the next morning—but still they wanted to lavish their time to get to know both me and Beate, my extraordinary translator from Germany. We were all sisters in one family, and that was the priority, not their schedules.

> If we value independence, convenience, and productivity more than inconvenient interdependence on and love for other human beings, we are outside of God's will. We've lost our vision of what this life is even *for*.

We live in a more time-harried culture. Many of us struggle with feeling like we don't have enough time. Whether we work away from home or remotely, we have meetings that won't change just because one of our kids left an important project at home and needs it run to school. Deadlines are real. Interruptions are inconvenient. We don't answer doorbells or phones. *Do not disturb* is a way of life. We have to be ruthless.

I worked remotely from home back in the '90s before it was a thing. I remember the pressure of needing to be a two-income family, with three children under the age of four, a husband who worked outside the home, my own demanding boss, and writing deadlines.

People talk about having a balanced life, but often we're not "balancing" work and family. One becomes far more important than the other. I think it makes more sense to think in terms of priorities. My priority at 3:00 p.m. was often different from the priority of my 9:00 a.m. meeting.

And if someone was bleeding, it all went out the window anyway.

I feel for people under similar or worse pressure today. I appreciate what my friends in their twenties, thirties, and forties go through. They have to work hard to swim in today's economy. What I see in them, and throughout the New Testament, is that each of us has to look to the Holy Spirit's guidance as to our individual time stewardship—and be willing to do God's will.

Stewardship is tough. Our time-crunched culture lures us toward some distant point in the future when we will arrive at the place where we can rest. (Culturally, this seems to mean that "we'll have enough"—enough money, prestige, power, and resources to do what we want.) So, the cultural drum beats on and on to the rhythm of personal advancement, and we row, row, row our boats. We rush toward accomplishing the next thing. Once x, y, and z are done, then I'll be free. No—then you'll be dead.

Some people, when they reach that mythical bliss of retirement, realize they wasted their lives in terms of what was important. They gain the whole world, so to speak, but lose the central priority that nourishes and satisfies: a relationship with God and relationships with other human beings.

This leads to another inconvenient challenge. To flourish, relationships demand that we be physically present.

As the coronavirus pandemic made clear, it is a wonderful

technological gift that we can connect virtually via the lovely digital devices we enjoy. Anyone who has spent hours on FaceTime with a new love who lives elsewhere gets that. So do grandparents who goo and coo and talk in a higher octave to their baby grandchildren who are far away. So do military spouses and everyone else who has loved ones who are physically distant.

Still, everyone would agree, there is no substitute for being physically together. It is how we were designed as human beings. Real connection flourishes in three-dimensional, flesh-and-blood interaction.

We see this not just in human relationships but in how God designed His whole story of creation, fall, redemption, and restoration. The Scriptures are not some collection of ephemeral spiritual ideas. They are, from beginning to end, a connected, historical story about real places and real events that happened to real people.

The story ends with the restoration of Eden's paradise in "a new heaven and a new earth," populated by people with actual resurrection bodies like Jesus' body, dancing with joy and drinking new wine.

It's no surprise that cultivating a flourishing relationship with God in this fallen world, just like connecting with other people, is terribly inconvenient.

Part of bonding with God is individual, of course. We spend time alone with Him, in eating the Word and digesting it in meditation, prayer, and praise. These spiritual disciplines, in solitude, are often the first thing that slides off our packed daily calendars.

While solitude is essential, we also need to be physically present with God in a fellowship of people whom we can see, hear, feel, smell, and touch, sharing the Lord's Supper, which we can actually taste.

But how can we physically be with Him? We can't see Him.

Jesus said, "For where two or three are gathered in my name, there am I among them."[54]

We experience the presence of God in His church, among His flesh-and-blood people, whom Jesus calls our brothers and sisters. In the Old Testament, God made His presence known in the temple: a physical place. In the New Testament, the apostle Paul reminded the church in Corinth that God's presence is now manifest in the church: "Do you not know that you are God's temple and that God's Spirit dwells in you? If anyone destroys God's temple, God will destroy him. For God's temple is holy, and you are that temple."[55]

The Greek word for "you" in these verses is *plural.* Paul was writing to a particular church in a particular place. Jesus followers, joined together in a local church family (even if they're dysfunctional—which we all are), are *the church*: a temple, a dwelling place for God's presence. So, Paul says, don't mess around. Be holy, as God is holy. And that is only possible through the Holy Spirit.

Mind-blowing.

God has designed this whole story of redemption so it is not just an individual thing, like, *Oh, yay, I come to Jesus, God is my copilot, and then I get to go upstairs when I die.* We are part of a covenant people declaring in word and deed the riches of His marvelous grace. We are part of the church Jesus started, but not just in a cosmic future sense. To track with His whole plan, we need to show up and be part of a local church community in real time.

And that's *really* inconvenient.

---

54 Matthew 18:20.

55 1 Corinthians 3:16-17.

Chapter 22

GO TO CHURCH!

But I know we can go slow and repair things in the ways that we can, in the places where we dwell, in the institutions we inhabit, with the people around us. We can serve the needy and the disadvantaged in our cities and towns. We can seek faithfulness in our small, local congregations. We can help form churches that are humble, accountable, and a radical alternative to the world, to both the political right and the political left.

TISH HARRISON WARREN, "Go Slow and Repair Things," *Christianity Today*

Go to church!

How's that for an action point?

I can't believe I'm even using this language. It sounds so pedantic. So 1950s-ish. As if going to church makes one tidy and religious and fully capable of flossing regularly and being a nice member of society. Check off that square church-attendance box, and you're done for the week.

I'm emboldened to use the phrase because there have always been lots of books and ads out there with verby titles that give us imperatives, like *Just Do It! Get Out of Your Head! Let Them! Eat Pray Love! Be All You Can Be! Eat Fresh! Think Different! Have It Your Way!*

I get that you may be thinking, "But who are you to tell me to go to church? You're not my mother!"

No, of course not, and please tell your mom hello for me, if you can.

I'm writing this because it's true. We need to go to church.

As this book's deadline drew near, I blocked off my usual schedule so I could concentrate on writing. And though I'm an active member of my local church, I would stay home on Sundays so I could work and "get more done." I'd watch the service later online.

I was aware of the irony. I told my friends, "I can't go to church because I'm writing this book about the vital importance of the local church!"

So, I'm writing to myself as well as to you.

I am aware of some of the minefields that bad church experiences create. I know that some churches are toxic and abusive or self-righteous or heretical. Flee any environment that tolerates these sins.

But not all churches are that way, and God designed us to live and breathe and grow in community. Church is not a smiley-face panacea dispensary. It's a body of individual Jesus followers doing life together in the midst of the complexities of today's world.

First, a caveat.

Some people can't go to church. I've interviewed people who've been in solitary conditions, unable to physically meet with other believers, and God met them there. Several brothers on death row. A Russian dissident imprisoned for her faith during Cold War days, held in a freezing solitary cell in Siberia. An American man held hostage by Middle Eastern extremists for more than a year. An officer whose faith grew while confined in the notorious "Hanoi Hilton" prison during the Vietnam War. The point is that those in enforced solitary confinement or medical isolation or receiving at-home care or with kids who are sick or have other special needs can, of course, know the communal power of the triune God without walking into a church.

> God designed us to live and breathe and grow in community.

But it's safe to say that most of us are not in those situations.

In 1938, while teaching at an underground seminary that had officially been closed by the Nazis, Dietrich Bonhoeffer wrote his book *Life Together*. (The Nazis executed Bonhoeffer in 1945.)

Reflecting on Christian community in a repressive regime, Bonhoeffer wrote:

> It is by the grace of God that a congregation is permitted to gather visibly in this world to share God's Word and sacrament. Not all Christians receive this blessing. The imprisoned, the sick, the scattered lonely, the proclaimers of the Gospel in [unbelieving] lands stand alone. They know that visible fellowship is a blessing.[u]

So, let's go to church. If you're not in one, find a good one.

Go where the community holds to one God, eternally existent in the Father, the Son, and the Holy Spirit. Go where the deity of Jesus Christ is preached, with the whole story: His virgin birth, His sinless life, His miracles, His atoning death through His blood, His bodily resurrection, His ascension to the right hand of the Father, and His personal return in power and glory.

Go to a church that preaches the Bible as the authoritative Word of God and the physical resurrection of believers in Jesus.

Go to a church that teaches the essential power of the Holy Spirit to regenerate sinful people and enable them, in unity, to follow Jesus and become more like Him.

If a church doesn't cleave to these distinctives, then it's lost touch with the New Testament church that Jesus started and has morphed into something else.

Don't go to a church because it has seats full of people you can relate to—people who are just like you. Don't go to a church because it can provide good business networking opportunities. Don't go because the speaker never says anything you don't like.

Prayerfully go to the church to which the Holy Spirit leads you.

And don't choose a church because it has good parking for a quick in and out, a coffee bar, or amazing vocals. Those are all great things, but as we've said, our convenience, control over our departure, and personal preference and desire to be comfortable are not usually spiritually healthy criteria by which to make decisions related to the care of our soul and our role within a beloved community.

Prayerfully go to the church to which the Holy Spirit leads you.

Being in community doesn't mean we're never alone. As I've said, the Spirit of God transforms and teaches us in solitude and meditation. But the fruits of our community can build up our times of solitude, and the fruits of solitude can build up our community.

So, show up. Pray with people. Be generous. Worship God. Laugh. Cry. Celebrate the Lord's Supper. Get baptized. Learn the Word.

It's not only a Sunday thing. Go further. Connect in a small group. Eat together. Eat a lot. Open your home or apartment or meet at a coffee shop. Open the Bible. Chew on it, pray through it, discuss it, learn from other humans, share your joys and sorrows. Repent in community. It's refreshing. These people are a mess. So are you. They're not always fun. Neither are you. But even as we connect with one another and listen, really listen, to other people's stories, something interesting can happen.

Researchers have found that when we engage in "active listening"—undistracted, empathetic absorption of a fellow human's words and body language—we experience "physiological synchronicity."[v] Unconsciously, our heart rate, breathing rate, and skin tones begin to match the other person's.

It's wild, as if we're one body or something.

Even as we take the simplest steps of obedience in choosing life together with other flawed followers of Jesus, something begins to happen if we are open to the working of the Spirit. (If we aren't, we'll just get frustrated and run out of gas.) Through the Spirit, in counterintuitive ways, God changes us *in community*. He gives us hope. We realize we're not the only one to struggle with certain things or feel certain ways. We get insights from other people's stories. We start to love them. We can gradually feel safe. Seen. Known.

And in all this, the Holy Spirit spurs us onward, always outward so that love in the body overflows to serve and include those who don't know Jesus. Help the poor. Seek justice. Serve those in any kind of need. Listen. Practice the virtue of neighboring.

We will encounter challenges along the way. No surprise there.

Ever since Jesus started His church, human beings have fallen short. And yet the church goes on, visible in flawed but redeemed communities all around this world. As we've seen, humble, individual churches do amazing things. They are light in the darkness of war-ravaged Ukraine. They bring food and help and love and compassion to their neighbors in the aftermath of disaster, like in Turkey. They bring fresh water and generous help and friendship to the poor in a dry land, like in Brazil. Forgiveness and comfort in the unthinkable, like in Rwanda and Egypt. Courage and perseverance in a hostile land, as in churches like Azad's in Turkey. Empowerment for the helpless, like in Uganda. They love the prisoner and the former terrorist and hang with them to help them build a new life and a ministry of their own, as with Tatiana in Tajikistan or Omer in Turkey.

Jesus is doing greater things through His people in the church He started around the world, including, yes, so many churches in the West. He works where He is wanted… and He will continue to do so as we follow Him together, until our part in His story ends.

Chapter 23

THE END OF THE STORY

After this I looked,
and behold,
a great multitude that no one could number,
from every nation, from all tribes and peoples
and languages,
standing before the throne and before the Lamb,
clothed in white robes, with palm branches
in their hands,
and crying out with a loud voice,

"Salvation belongs to our God who sits on the throne,
and to the Lamb!"

And all the angels were standing around the throne
and around the elders and the four living creatures,
and they fell on their faces before the throne
and worshiped God, saying,

"Amen! Blessing and glory
and wisdom and thanksgiving and honor
and power and might
be to our God forever and ever! Amen."
(Revelation 7:9-12)

Amen and amen.

IF YOU ARE CURIOUS ABOUT ICM...

Millions of our fellow believers around the world don't have a secure, permanent place to gather in and worship. Their congregations meet under trees, in shacks, or in other unsafe conditions, vulnerable to monsoons, severe heat or cold, attrition and social persecution. The lack of a church home also hinders their ability to spread the gospel and disciple new believers.

International Cooperating Ministries' process of church development begins with an established, local congregation recommended by carefully vetted in-country ministry partners. (The ministry currently works with 300 such partners, and they are like the first-century heroes of the faith.) ICM connects their need with donor resources in the West, providing high-quality building materials and translated Bible resources otherwise out of reach for many under-resourced pastors and their congregations.

Then the local congregation provides the land and the sweat equity, transforming the project from a handout into a deeply rooted, cooperative accomplishment.

Such permanent, legally recognized churches become centers for discipleship, safe havens for believers to gather in, and launching pads for wider service and outreach. These hubs often attract resources from other organizations—including Samaritan's Purse, Hope International and Compassion International—to provide clean water, feeding programs, saving Clubs, and job training. Each congregation commits to evangelism and church planting upon completion of their construction. God uses all this to transform individuals, families, and whole communities.

As I write, this partnership between believers in the West and believers in less developed countries has built more than 14,000 churches, Hope Centers, training facilities, and Christian schools. ICM has equipped these congregations with translated Bible study materials now in use by more than 26 million people. Since 1986, ICM has been connecting believers in the global church with their brothers and sisters in Christ who can give—just like the churches in the book of Acts. The result of that partnership is accelerating the gospel, resourcing churches in the hardest-to-reach places, and transforming struggling villages into thriving, Jesus-following communities—one church at a time.

Learn more at www.icm.org!

ENDNOTES

a C.S. Lewis, *The Screwtape Letters* (Macmillan, 1982), p. 56.

b J.I. Packer, *Concise Theology: A Guide to Historic Christian Beliefs* (Tyndale, 1993), p. 194.

c C.S. Lewis quoted in *The Collected Letters of C.S. Lewis, Vol. III: Narnia, Cambridge and Joy, 1950-1963*, edited by Walter Hooper (Harper, 2007), p. 68-69.

d C.S. Lewis, *Mere Christianity* (Macmillan, 1960), p. 47.

e Encyclopaedia Britannica. "Nubia." Accessed February 12, 2026. https://www.britannica.com/place/Nubia.

f Shavkat Ikromov, "Mosque Diplomacy in Central Asia: Geopolitics Beginning with the Mihrab," Voices on Central Asia, https://voicesoncentralasia.org/mosque-diplomacy-in-central-asia-geopolitics-beginning-with-the-mihrab/ (accessed February 12, 2026).

g Silja Fröhlich, "Iran, Turkey, Saudi Arabia Build Africa Mosques," Deutsche Welle, December 18, 2019, https://www.dw.com/en/mosques-in-africa-a-test-of-strength-in-the-middle-east/a-51717439 (accessed February 12, 2026)

h R. Cavanaugh, "Turkey's Christians Face the Future with Reasons for Hope, Caution," International Christian Concern, January 28, 2026, https://persecution.org/2026/01/28/turkeys-christians-face-the-future-with-reasons-for-hope-caution/ (accessed February 12, 2026).

i Hollie Nyseth Nzitatira, Trey Billing, and Jared F. Edgerton, "How Radio Affects Violent Conflict: New Evidence from Rwanda," American Sociological Review 89, no. 5 (2024): 876–906, https://journals.sagepub.com/doi/10.1177/00031224241278905 (accessed February 12, 2026).

j A version of this story appeared in *Christianity Today*: Ellen Vaughn, "He Defended His Family's Murderer" *Christianity Today*. www.christianitytoday.com/2025/01/rwanda-forgiveness-he-befriended-familys-murderer/ (accessed December 1, 2025).

k A version of this story appeared in *Christianity Today*: Ellen Vaughn "A River (of Aid) Runs Through It" *Christianity Today* www.christianitytoday.com/2025/01/ukraine-christians-river-of-aid-runs-through-it/ (accessed December 1, 2025).

l Alaa Al Aswany, "Egypt's Two-Front War for Democracy," *The New York Times*, November 10, 2013, https://www.nytimes.com/2013/11/11/opinion/aswani-egypts-two-front-war-for-democracy.html.

m "May God Forgive the ISIS Killers," www.schwebster.org/sermons/sermon-archives/2015-sermons/may-god-forgive-the-isis-killers (accessed on December 1, 2025).

n "The Digital Day: New Survey Reveals Americans Spend Over 10 Hours Online," August 28, 2025, www.optimum.com/articles/internet/americans-spend-10-hours-daily-online-survey (accessed on December 1, 2025).

o E.J. Newman, N. Schwarz, "Misinformed by images: How images influence perceptions of truth and what can be done about it," December 3, 2023, https://pubmed.ncbi.nlm.nih.gov/38134526/ (accessed on December 1, 2025).

p John Calvin, *The Institutes of the Christian Religion*, https://www.ccel.org/ccel/calvin/institutes.toc.html (accessed on December 1, 2025).

q C.S. Lewis, *The Screwtape Letters*, (Macmillan, 1982), p. 56.

r Marshall Segal, "Let the Lukewarm Come to Me," May 31, 2021, www.desiringgod.org/articles/let-the-lukewarm-come-to-me, (accessed on December 1, 2025).

s *A Path Through Suffering: Discovering the Relationship Between God's Mercy and Our Pain* (Regal, 2003), p. #.

t Amy Carmichael, *Mountain Breezes: The Collected Poems of Amy Carmichael*, (CLC Publications, 1999), 293.

u Dietrich Bonhoeffer, *Life Together*, (HarperOne, 2009), p. 18.

v L.S. Escobar, M. Robbins, J. Hwang, S.M. Jung, D.J. Park, "Exploring cardiac physiological synchrony and its implications for stress and anxiety," *Ageing and Neurodegenerative Diseases*, 2025; 5:21, https://dx.doi.org/10.20517/and.2025.14 (accessed on December 1, 2025).